GOSPEL
on the
MOUNTAINS

ALSO BY BILL CROWDER

Available for God's Purpose
Before Christmas
For This He Came
God of Surprise
Let's Talk
Living with Courage
Moving Beyond Failure
My Hope Is in You
One Thing Is Necessary
Overcoming Life's Challenges
Seeing the Heart of Christ
The Spotlight of Faith
Trusting God in Hard Times
Windows on Christmas
Windows on Easter

Devotionals
A Compassionate Heart
A Deep Dependence
A Present Peace

GOSPEL
on the
MOUNTAINS

Nine Encounters
with God from the Bible

BILL
CROWDER

Our Daily Bread
Publishing™

CONTENTS

Acknowledgments........................ 9

Introduction: A Mountaintop Experience 11

1. Mount Ararat: A Second Chance 15

2. Mount Moriah: A Promise Kept 31

3. Mount Sinai: The Law Is Given............ 49

4. Mount Nebo: Choices and Consequences 63

5. Mount Zion: A Home for the King......... 79

6. Mount Carmel: An Invitation to Return 93

7. Mount of Teaching: Life in the Kingdom 107

8. Mount of Transfiguration: Father and Son ... 125

9. "Mount" Calvary: Love on Display 141

Conclusion: Go, Tell It on the Mountains....... 155

ACKNOWLEDGMENTS

For many people, recent years have been a time spent in the valley—perhaps even "the valley of the shadow of death" (Psalm 23:4). During the days of COVID-19's isolation and quarantining, my ninety-five-year-old mom—Bee Crowder—passed away. That season of loss was exacerbated, as it was for so many other families during those difficult days, by our family having to wait 135 days to have any kind of memorial service at which we could honor her memory and comfort one another. Our experience was, in a sense, not unique, but it was ours—and we all felt the weight of it.

One of the many things I remember and appreciate about my mom was that she was always one of my best first readers of the books I wrote. Even in her later years, her sharp mind would catch (and challenge) logical inconsistencies, identify punctuation and grammar problems, and generally test whatever I had written with the very best kind of critical reading. While I miss Mom in so many ways, as I have worked on this project, I particularly miss her wise, trusted input. She has had a profound, valuable impact on so much of my writing. I really do hope that she would have liked this one as well.

With the loss of Mom's participation, it makes me lean even harder on the team at Our Daily Bread Publishing who have gladly invested themselves in this project. Our new publisher, Chriscynethia Floyd, has been an encourager, along with Dawn Anderson, ODBP's executive editor. As always, I am thankful for the help and partnership of my editor, Dave

Branon, who, a brilliant writer in his own stead, provided wise counsel and appropriate pushback to make this a study that will, I trust, be an encouragement and challenge to all who read it. Add to that our marketing team, led by Londa Alderink and moved forward by John Van Der Veen and Marjie Johnson. I was recently approached by an author who'd had a very disappointing time with another publisher and wanted to know about my experience with ODBP. On the back of years of working with this group, I could only tell him how grateful I am for these friends and their great work. I could not ask for a better team to work with on a book like this.

Now that we are empty nesters, my wife, Marlene, is the helper at home who endures the long process of writing and contributes needed encouragement when the going is a bit rough. As we approach forty-five years of marriage together, I could not imagine a better life partner or one more patient with the emotional ups and downs that go along with writing.

As always, however, my greatest thanks is for the One who made the mountains and then used them as one of His tools for telling His story. As John put it, "All things came into being through Him, and apart from Him not even one thing came into being that has come into being" (John 1:3). That includes not only the mountains He created but also the powerful events that happened on their peaks. This is the story of Jesus Christ told from the perspective of the mountains, and my desire is that as we explore those events together He will be honored above and beyond anything and everything He has made.

A Mountaintop Experience

Masada.

On my first trip leading a study group to Israel, I enjoyed just about everything we did and saw and experienced. But all along the way I was anticipating one day in particular—the day when I would stand where the Roman general Lucius Flavius Silva stood, contemplating Herod's ancient mountaintop fortress at Masada. Our bus pulled into the parking lot, and our group joined the hundreds of other tourists in the queue to ride the tram up to the summit of the mountain for a time of exploration and reflection.

I had a different plan for my visit. Leaving the group to ride the tram, I began to make my way up the long "snake path"—a winding footpath along the side of the mountain. When I reached the top (forty-five minutes later), I sat at the edge of the plateau pondering the view of the Dead Sea and the wasteland surrounding it, and I considered the momentous events that had happened on that spot. There, in the early 70s AD, a group of Jewish freedom fighters, women, and children stood off the siege strategy of Silva's Tenth Legion for months.

Tragically, those Jewish zealots would ultimately commit suicide rather than fall into the hands of their Roman enemies. But their stand was not forgotten. In fact, the modern state of Israel is determined that it will *never* be forgotten. Still today, newly trained Israeli Defense Forces troops take their oath of service at the top of Masada, ending their verbal commitment with the determined cry that Masada will never fall again.

The mountain tells the story.

Growing up in the West Virginia mountains, I learned to love their beauty. And from several years of working on a survey crew for pipelines, maps, and well location sites all over those mountains, I also know that, like Masada, those mountains have a story to tell. In West Virginia, the mountains tell of hardscrabble existence and close-knit families that have learned to survive a very difficult life—sometimes at great cost.

The Rocky Mountains, with their "purple mountain majesties," tell their own story—a story of determined pilgrims traveling to the west with aspirations of meaningful opportunities not available to them in the places they had left behind, and of the Native Americans who had roamed that region for centuries.

The South American Andes form the backdrop for the story of the Incas, a powerful culture capable of producing Machu Picchu, the Peruvian mountain fortress that today is one of Peru's most popular tourist sites.

The rugged Caucasus Mountains form, in a sense, the point of demarcation for the continental division between Asia and Europe—and it has been for centuries a nexus for conflict between the racially and religiously divided peoples there.

All these mountains I have seen. Each is spectacular in its own way. Each has a story to tell—and that is true of the mountains in the Bible as well. Certainly, much of the Bible's story occurs on the plains, but those flatlands are overshadowed by the famous mountains whose names we can easily recite—Ararat, Moriah, Carmel, Olivet, and more. There is a distinct pattern in the Scriptures that, time after time, some of the most important events in the Bible's story get told on the mountains of the Bible lands.

> Some of the most important events in the Bible's story get told on the mountains of the Bible lands.

What makes this fascinating is that the Bible appears to have something of a love-hate relationship with those high places. In Psalm 121:1–2, we read:

> I will raise my eyes to the mountains;
> From where will my help come?
> My help comes from the LORD,
> Who made heaven and earth.

The first half of that statement seems to speak of the ancient practice of worshipping false gods and idols on high places—hilltops and mountains. Repeatedly, when the Southern Kingdom of Judah had a king who was committed to the things of Yahweh, the true and living God of Israel, the first thing that new king did was to tear down the high places. Why? The second half of the verse provides the critical response: "My help comes from the LORD, who made heaven and earth."

From the Lord.

Not the mountains.

Not the gods of the mountains.

The One who made the mountains.

Part of the Songs of Ascent, sung by Jewish pilgrims as they made their way to Jerusalem for the high feast times, Psalm 121 was a reminder to look higher than the mountains to the God of Abraham, Isaac, and Jacob. Yet, as we will discover together, the God who made the mountains and is greater than the mountains has seen fit to use the mountains as a setting for some of the most significant events in the Scriptures, providing important momentum to the overall story of the Bible.

As we move through the Scriptures from Genesis on through to the days of Jesus, we see God telling His story— and we see how He has lovingly met our deep spiritual need with His extravagant supply. Join me as we scale the heights of God's work in His world—His message on the mountains.

1

MOUNT ARARAT

A Second Chance

It is safe to say that Louis Washkansky is not exactly a household name. In December of 1967, Louis was a fifty-four-year-old grocer who underwent the first successful heart transplant operation. While Dr. Christiaan Barnard, who performed that surgery, became instantly famous, the lesser-known Washkansky lived for an additional eighteen days with his new heart. Though he did not survive for years and years, his brief survival validated the transplant process and led to further medical advances in cardiovascular research and surgical techniques that have offered countless others real hope for longer life.

Tommy John was an American baseball pitcher whose Major League career was solid, if unspectacular. Yet to this day his name is constantly referred to in baseball circles for something other than his pitching. While pitching for the Los Angeles Dodgers, John suffered a tear in the ulnar collateral ligament in his pitching arm—an injury that threatened to end his career. Into this time of uncertainty stepped Dr. Frank Jobe with a brand-new, revolutionary, and experimental surgical method. He repaired the damaged arm with this procedure, and John returned to baseball, his career extended by the daring operation. "Tommy John surgery" instantly became an enduring part of the sports landscape, and like John, scores of baseball players have enjoyed extended careers that, without this surgery, they would likely have never had.

In Stone County, Arkansas, Terry Wallis's automotive accident left one person killed and Wallis in a coma. That was in 1984. On June 11, 2003, however, Wallis miraculously emerged from the coma to be the longest coma survivor in history. That record is also held by a railroad worker who was sent into a coma by a brain tumor. Like Wallis, Jan Grzebski of Poland emerged from his coma after nineteen years.

Aside from the medical miracles present in each of these cases, these events have something simpler in common. Against all odds, these individuals experienced a second chance at life or, in Tommy John's case, at his career. So many times, second chances are extraordinary. For some who experience these fresh starts, they make all the difference in their stories.

What we have seen in the medical realm is true of some well-known second-chance events in the Bible as well. In fact, some of the most beloved characters in Scripture might have never achieved such a lofty status had they not been granted a second chance.

- Joseph experienced a second chance in Egypt after being falsely imprisoned, and rose to a position of authority equivalent to that of prime minister of Egypt.

- David received a second chance to retain his rule over Israel following his moral failure with Bathsheba and his conflict with Absalom.

- Simon Peter was given a second chance at following Jesus after his fear-filled denials of Christ in a courtyard by a charcoal fire.

- John Mark received a second chance at serving his Lord after deserting Paul and Barnabas on one of their first missionary journeys.

As we likewise find ourselves sometimes needing a second chance, it is encouraging to see that with our loving God second chances are very much available. But, as we will see, not only did many individuals in the Scriptures receive second chances, the entire human race has been given numerous second chances. And one of the most significant of those second chances happened on a mountain.

A First Chance Wasted

Perhaps the only thing better than getting a second chance is not needing one, because the first chance was embraced and responded to in the right way. Back in 1925, Major League baseball player Lou Gehrig got the opportunity to start at first base for the New York Yankees instead of the normal first-choice first baseman, Wally Pipp. Years later, Pipp maintained that he had been removed from the lineup because he had been hit in the head by a pitched ball during batting practice. Gehrig grabbed the opportunity with both hands and didn't let go until he had played in 2,130 consecutive games—earning him the nickname "The Iron Horse."

The human race, however, wasted its first chance (and many others as well). When the Creator first made people, He placed human beings in a perfect environment, which our first parents lost through their disobedience (see Genesis 3). Covered with animal skins, they exited their Edenic paradise to make their way in the wider world—and what followed was, putting it mildly, catastrophic. The first brothers created the first sibling rivalry, resulting in the first murder—and things went downhill from there. The Scriptures provide two significant pieces of information to show how the fallen race spread and how far those people truly fell from the created state of their first parents:

The genealogy (Genesis 5) that tracks the record of the faithful from Adam to Noah by way of Enoch

The description of the depths of depravity (Genesis 6) to which the human race sunk

As we enter Genesis 6, we encounter a mysterious description of intimate encounters between the "sons of God" and the "daughters of mankind"—a conversation that is beyond our scope here. However, what we can see is that, whatever that text is describing, it is a situation that feeds into the dark condition of the human race described in verse 5:

Then the LORD saw that the wickedness of mankind was great on the earth, and that every intent of the thoughts of their hearts was only evil continually.

Created as image bearers of God, men and women had become a faint mockery of the intent of their Creator. With human brokenness having reached full flower, the Bible's stark description of that fallenness is stunning in its honest simplicity. Of particular significance is the intensity of the words used to describe the condition of humanity at this moment in history:

Wickedness.

Every intent only evil.

Continually.

Add to that the words of verse 11, "Now the earth was corrupt in the sight of God, and the earth was filled with violence," and verse 12, "God looked on the earth, and behold, it was corrupt; for all humanity had corrupted its way upon the earth." Taken together, those verses confront us with comprehensive corruption and pervasive evil that desecrated God's perfect creation.

The pointed words used in these texts describe systemic, continual, intentional rebellion against the creator God, apparently resulting in savage treatment of people for one another (perhaps implied in the word *wickedness*) and prompting a chilling reaction from God himself—a response that had two parts, both of which could cause us to scratch our heads.

First, we are told in verse 6 that "the LORD was sorry that He had made mankind on the earth, and He was grieved in His heart." Some wonder at this, trying to figure out whether it implies that God thought He had made a mistake in creating humankind. If you accept the consistent testimony of Scripture, then you must come to the conclusion that God does not make mistakes. By definition, everything the all-wise God does is right. So what is in view here?

Some scholars refer to God's sorrow over His creative work as an *anthropopathism*. What is that?

The Bible refers to God as spirit, yet at times the Scriptures use physical human characteristics to enable us to understand something about Him. So, we read about the "eyes of the Lord" or the "hand of the Lord" or the "arm of the Lord." As spirit, God doesn't literally have eyes or hands or arms, but those word pictures help us understand Him. These expressions are called *anthropomorphisms*, which comes from two Greek words meaning "human form"—where the invisible God is described in visible ways.

Similarly, Isaiah 55 reminds us that God's ways are higher than our ways and His thoughts are higher than our thoughts. So, how can we begin to understand such an inscrutable God? To help us with that, sometimes the Bible uses the aforementioned anthropopathisms (which comes from two Greek words meaning "human feelings"). These descriptors relate the heart of God in human terms to give us a point of reference as to how God feels about certain things. Here in Genesis 6, though God doesn't make mistakes, He is described as having the kind of sorrow a human would have if they, in fact, did make a mistake.

More important to me, however, is that God is described as being grieved. This is an emotion the Scriptures tell us God *does* experience. This grief and heartbrokenness over the condition of the human race is so severe, so pervasive, so extreme that it demands a divine response—and that brings us to the second part of God's reaction to human sin that could prompt head-scratching:

The LORD said, "I will wipe out mankind whom I have created from the face of the land; mankind, and animals as well, and crawling things, and the birds of the sky. For I am sorry that I have made them." (v. 7)

Many in our generation struggle with that. "How could a loving God obliterate the human race?" they ask. Theologians have wrestled with that very question, not only in this text but also in other Old Testament events—prompting some to say that the God of the Old Testament is a different God from what we discover in Jesus in the New Testament. Yet, while God's intent to cleanse His creation may trouble some people, we must remember that, first and foremost, this is His creation. He is sovereign over it. He, as a holy God, has the right to enact judgment at any moment in history that He chooses to. He is God.

We may not understand this. We may not even like it. But if we accept the Bible's description of God, we must also accept the fact that since God does not make mistakes, nothing He does is wrong. By definition of His perfect nature, we accept that God's ways are beyond us and rest in the words of Abraham in Genesis 18:25, "Shall not the Judge of all the earth deal justly?" Yes, He will always do right, though we may not always understand the rightness of it.

Grace is the stuff of which second chances are made.

The human race had seemingly reached a point of irretrievable sinfulness. But there was hope for humanity. There was hope because, although God is a God of justice, He is also a God of grace. The Scriptures describe God not only as all wise and always right but also as merciful and faithful:

> The LORD, the LORD God, compassionate and merciful, slow to anger, and abounding in faithfulness and truth; who keeps faithfulness for thousands, who forgives wrongdoing, violation of His Law, and sin; yet He will by no means leave the guilty unpunished. (Exodus 34:6–7)

God is merciful, but He still deals with sin. The world received judgment, but as we will see, one man named Noah and his family found grace—and what began as a season of judgment resolved into a second chance for the human race. That's because grace is the stuff of which second chances are made.

A Vehicle of Grace

I was about twenty years old and had not yet come to faith in Christ when a coworker invited me to his church to see the film *In Search of Noah's Ark*. I had grown up going to Sunday school and had heard the story of the flood (and seen the flannelgraphs) more than once. Still, I was intrigued by the idea that the ark might actually exist. Though I didn't really gain any great new knowledge about the ark from the film, I did find a new curiosity that led me to continue attending that church. It was an early step in my coming to Christ.

That curiosity and interest in the ark was not limited to me or to a time in the early 1970s. Anthropologists and missionaries tell us that many cultures around the world have stories of an ancient flood and an ark of deliverance. Today, ongoing fascination with the story of Noah's ark is evidenced in the scores of people who daily visit Ark Encounter, a to-scale reproduction of Noah's ark in Williamstown, Kentucky. The story of Noah seems to never grow old.

In Genesis 6, in the midst of humanity's sinfulness and God's grief, we read that "Noah found grace in the eyes of the LORD" (v. 8 NKJV). The imminent judgment of God was mitigated by rescue. In the following verses, we see God's intentionality in giving humanity a way back from their corruption. And that way back focused on one man and his family.

What do we know about him?

His name. While the source of the name *Noah* is debated, its core meaning is rooted in the idea of comfort and rest. Certainly that name is appropriate, as God would bring rest and restoration to His spoiled creation through this man.

His character. Genesis 6:9 says, "Noah was a righteous man, blameless in his generation. Noah walked with God." Interestingly, Noah's great-grandfather was Enoch, whose life was so pleasing to God that he entered the presence of God without having to face death (5:24; see also Hebrews 11:5). This example may have influenced Noah to be the man that he was; like Enoch, Noah "walked with God." The result of that walk was that Noah's life was marked as "righteous" and "blameless." A man of high character because he walked in relationship with his God, Noah personified an Old Testament example of a grace-filled life.

His family. Noah was aided in his ark-building project and accompanied on that ark by his wife, his three sons (Ham, Shem, Japheth), and their wives. From this modest family came God's divinely appointed rescue—and humanity's second chance.

So, the consequences of humankind's corruption were fully realized, but through one man and his family, God offered a fresh opportunity to the world. As recorded in Genesis 7, the heavens opened, the deeps erupted, and the resulting flood overwhelmed the world in a way that accomplished God's purposes of bringing to bear the consequences of humankind's sinful choices.

The Expositor's Bible Commentary gives an overview of the scope of the event, told by the author of Genesis in the form of a chiasm. A *chiasm* is a Hebrew device for storytelling that maps the events in parallel form, following the shape of the Greek letter chi, or *X*. The flood story unfolds below:

7 days of waiting for flood (7:4)
  7 days of waiting for flood (7:10)
    40 days of flood (7:17a)
      150 days of water triumphing (7:24)
      150 days of water waning (8:3)
    40 days of waiting (8:6)
  7 days of waiting (8:10)
7 days of waiting (8:12)

That chiasm ends with Noah, his family, and the animals on board the ark, waiting. There, on the ark, the little family waited. And wondered.

Perhaps not even fully aware of the extent to which the flood had done its work.

Perhaps not yet understanding how empty the world now was.

Perhaps wondering if the promised second chance would come at all.

But it would come . . . and it would come on a mountain.

A Place for a Second Chance

After the dark despair of Genesis 6, the broken reality of the human race, and the jarring consequences that formed God's response to that condition in Genesis 7, the light begins to shine again. Notice how Genesis 8 opens:

> But God remembered Noah and all the animals and all the livestock that were with him in the ark; and God caused a wind to pass over the earth, and the water subsided. (v. 1)

What relief lives in those words! "God remembered Noah." And with judgment having done its work, rescue is now underway:

> Also the fountains of the deep and the floodgates of the sky were closed, and the rain from the sky was restrained; and the water receded steadily from the earth, and at the end of 150 days the water decreased. Then in the seventh month, on the seventeenth day of the month, the ark rested upon the mountains of Ararat. (vv. 2–4)

Now, as the waters subside, the ark comes to rest on Mount Ararat. What do we know about that place? *The New Bible Commentary* says, first of all, that "*Ararat* is not specifically modern Mt. Ararat but the territory of ancient Urartu, which is roughly modern Armenia and adjacent areas in Turkey and Iran."

The New Manners and Customs of the Bible also provides some helpful information here, though it does identify modern Mount Ararat as the biblical peak by the same name:

Mount Ararat consists of two volcanic peaks in extreme eastern Turkey, near the border with Armenia and Iran, on which the ark rested after the Flood subsided. . . . The Persian people call it *Koh-i-nuh*, "Noah's Mountain," and have a legend that refers to Ararat as the cradle of the human race.

From the lowlands of the Aras River, Ararat rises to a height of nearly 17,000 feet. It has two conical peaks: Little Ararat and Great Ararat.

"Noah's Mountain" is an important designation for Ararat because it connects the mountain to the biblical story of the flood and humankind's second chance. Ararat is mentioned three other times in the Bible, but only here is it described as a mountain, or mountain range. Impressive though this mountain may be, the reality of the location feels secondary to the significance and meaning of what happened there and what that location represents. That representation began in verse 1, where "God remembered Noah." Then, with verses 3 and 4, the page turns and restoration of life on earth begins, giving the human race a second chance—and that is what I think of when I think of Ararat.

Every mountain in the Bible has its own story to tell, and when I think of Mount Ararat in particular, I think of the fresh start that began there. A second chance for a wayward race to start over with their God. Genesis 8:17 clearly expresses that second chance when, as Noah and his family exit the ark, God instructs them to "be fruitful and multiply on the earth" (NKJV).

There it is. The first chance was offered to Adam and Eve in Genesis 1:28, which reads, "God blessed them; and God

said to them, 'Be fruitful and multiply, and fill the earth.'"
Now, on Mount Ararat, Noah and his family receive those
same words, commissioning them to reboot what Adam and
Eve had started—but whose failure had marked the world so
darkly.

Now humankind gets another chance. A fresh start. And,
while the Scriptures, human history, and our own experience prove unequivocally that there were a seemingly endless
number of failures yet to come—beginning with Noah's own
failings in Genesis 9—this second chance carried a powerful
promise. God said:

> This is the sign of the covenant which I am making
> between Me and you and every living creature that
> is with you, for all future generations; I have set My
> rainbow in the cloud, and it shall serve as a sign of
> a covenant between Me and the earth. It shall come
> about, when I make a cloud appear over the earth,
> that the rainbow will be seen in the cloud, and I will
> remember My covenant, which is between Me and you
> and every living creature of all flesh; and never again
> shall the water become a flood to destroy all flesh.
> When the rainbow is in the cloud, then I will look at
> it, to remember the everlasting covenant between God
> and every living creature of all flesh that is on the earth.
> (9:12–16)

Yes, humanity would continue to fail, and God would
continue to bring to them the consequences of those failures—but never again would those consequences include
the type of global cataclysm seen in the flood. And second
chances became a common theme in the biblical story:

After the Tower of Babel, God gave a second chance through Abraham.

After Sarah's manipulation through Hagar, a second chance was granted to Sarah as God gave her a son, Isaac.

After four hundred years in slavery for the Israelites, God brought a second chance through Moses.

After Moses's failures in the wilderness, God gave a second chance through Joshua.

After Israel's idolatry, Deborah's leadership was the vehicle for a second chance for the nation.

After Saul, God gave a second chance through David.

After Baal, God gave a second chance through Elijah.

And on and on and on.

All of these second chances echo God's grace to Noah on Mount Ararat. God offered a second chance, and the human race began again.

Grace and Truth

When I was in Bible college, one of my profs liked to say, "All of God's acts of judgment are ultimately acts of mercy." While judgment is certainly on display in the events of the flood, the second chance given to the human race was also a powerful display of mercy. This speaks profoundly of the heart of our God as displayed in Jesus, for in John 1:17 we read:

For the Law was given through Moses; grace and truth were realized through Jesus Christ.

Notice that while Jesus came bringing grace, He also championed truth. Our good God must let truth prevail, yet He consistently reminds of His mercies. Lamentations 3:22–23 reminds us:

The Lord's acts of mercy indeed do not end,
For His compassions do not fail.
They are new every morning;
Great is Your faithfulness.

While our unwise choices will always generate the consequences that truth demands, we can also be sure of God's heart for us. It is out of that heart—filled with unfailing compassions and new mercies—that second chances come, because as God is faithful to His own truth-filled character, He is also faithful to His grace-based promises to us.

As God is faithful to His own truth-filled character, He is also faithful to His grace-based promises to us.

As I reflect on that, I find myself being thankful. I am thankful for God's loving discipline that corrects my wrong behavior, and I'm thankful for the second, third, fourth, and more chances to walk with Him afresh. Just as Noah strode down Mount Ararat to begin humanity's second chance to walk with God, I am invited back by my forgiving Father to walk with Him and become more of the person He longs for me to be.

Second chances are God's ultimate response to us when we fail—for that is what grace is all about. As Annie J. Flint so beautifully put it:

When we have exhausted our store of endurance,
When our strength has failed ere the day is half done,
When we reach the end of our hoarded resources
Our Father's full giving is only begun.

His love has no limits, His grace has no measure,
His power no boundary known unto men;
For out of His infinite riches in Jesus
He giveth, and giveth, and giveth again.

A Promise Kept

In 1968, a new Broadway musical based on a book by Neil Simon launched, featuring the music of award-winning composer Burt Bacharach. The name of the musical was *Promises, Promises*, and Bacharach's score was upbeat and lively—but that score failed to give a clear picture of the play's basic story. It was not merely about promises—it was about promises being broken on a tragically consistent basis. Specifically, it was about husbands who regularly betrayed the trust of their wives by breaking their wedding vows. Clearly, not all promises are kept.

On May 7, 1977, Marlene and I made promises to each other and our married journey began. All these years later, our marriage has endured. It has not always been easy. It has not always been perfect. It has not always been hearts and flowers. There have been plenty of frustrations and disappointments along the way. On both sides. But with the Lord's help, we have endeavored to keep our promises to each other—and at times it was commitment to those promises that kept us on course. So, it is also clear that not all promises are broken.

But promises are a tough needle to thread. In fact, in the 1990s, during the peak of the Promise Keepers Christian men's movement, I heard one man say that he wasn't sure he even qualified to attend a Promise Keepers rally. He said, tongue in cheek (I hope), that he was waiting for someone to begin a "Promise Breakers" movement—for that he felt eminently qualified. Maybe that has been your experience. Or perhaps it has been the experience of people you love and for whom you hurt. It seems that broken marital promises especially result in deep and abiding pain that is not easily remedied.

Though the previous examples focus on marriage promises, we all know that promises factor in to just about every area of life. We are constantly confronted by promises of all different kinds and from a variety of sources:

Promises from candidates for office during election campaigns

Promises from advertisers for the next must-have product that, in the end, may or may not perform as advertised

Promises from employers who then award the promotion and the raise to someone else

Promises, promises

If you have experienced broken promises (and I'm guessing you have experienced that kind of disappointment more than once), they can cause a person to become cynical. Skeptical. They can cause us to automatically doubt the truthfulness of almost anyone and anything—and that is a really sad way to live. The truth is that, while we should never be foolish or naive, we should also never allow ourselves to become jaded.

So, when you have been repeatedly burned by broken promises, how do you ever find it possible to believe a promise again? What constitutes the indisputable solid ground on which a promise can be trusted? I would suggest to you that trust is ultimately rooted in one thing: *the trustworthiness of the person making the promise.*

> Trust is ultimately rooted in one thing: *the trustworthiness of the person making the promise.*

That is why marketing firms spend extraordinary amounts of time and money to recruit spokespersons they think people will trust, testing potential representatives in focus groups and surveys based on the demographic they are trying to reach. Is the person likable? Believable? Compatible? Suitable for the company, service, or product being advertised? All that effort to answer one question: Will the consumer trust him or her? You see, it really is that simple. The trustworthiness of the promise is founded on the trustworthiness of the promise maker.

This idea of trust and promises brings us back to our exploration of mountains in the Bible. We travel forward in the book of Genesis to see a shocking moment on a mountain that is all about a promise—and the God we can trust to keep His promises.

A Promise Given

There wasn't anything necessarily wrong or decidedly bad in the church where I was pastoring, but, in one particular season of ministry, there were little things that felt big and unspoken things that seemed loud. I was struggling to read the meaning behind these conflicting emotions, but I was certain about one thing—I felt uncomfortable and unsettled. Discussing these unwelcome emotions with a friend, he challenged me to consider a different possibility. "What if," he said, "this is God's way of loosening your roots? Of getting you ready to make a move for which you are not yet prepared?" That counsel struck me as odd, but I took it to heart and began to see these little changes as preparations for a bigger change. Change produces changes.

This seems to have been the case for the ancient patriarch Abram (who would become better known as Abraham). Having traveled with his extended family from their home in Ur of the Chaldeans to a new country called Haran, Abram must have thought that they had found a good place to settle down and build a home. But change produces changes, and when Abram's father died (Genesis 11:32), it set the stage for a bigger move than the one they'd already taken. Abram, now seventy-five years old, was to discover that Haran was not his true destination, for God himself would move him onward.

Genesis 12:1–3 records both the change coming to Abram, and the promise God attached to that change:

Now the LORD said to Abram,

"Go from your country,
And from your relatives

And from your father's house,
To the land which I will show you;
And I will make you into a great nation,
And I will bless you,
And make your name great;
And you shall be a blessing;
And I will bless those who bless you,
And the one who curses you I will curse.
And in you all the families of the earth will be blessed."

This change was not small. Having already left his homeland and then having subsequently lost his father, Abram was challenged by God to walk away from the bulk of his remaining family and launch out into unknown territory—what God called "the land which I will show you." *The New Bible Commentary* rightly describes the size of God's challenge to Abram:

> Leaving homeland and family was a much greater decision in a traditional society than in today's mobile, individualistic culture. Abram risked everything he held most dear to obey God's call.

In our world, moving from place to place is just part of our culture. A lack of roots is considered the cost of doing business. Not so in Abram's time. People were rooted in two things: land and family. God's instructions to Abram demanded that he distance himself from both.

That tremendous challenge—and the change it represented—becomes even clearer with a simple question: Was this Abram's first time to hear from God? Ur, his homeland, was home to a variety of gods, and this is the first time the

biblical text records Abram encountering the one true God—
an encounter that can only be understood as an act of God's
grace. Pastor and teacher Warren Wiersbe wrote:

> God called Abraham out of idolatry (Joshua 24:2)
> when he was in Ur of the Chaldees (Gen. 11:28, 31;
> 15:7; Nehemiah 9:7), a city devoted to Nannar, the
> moon-god. Abraham did not know the true God and
> had done nothing to deserve knowing Him, but God
> graciously called him.

God graciously called Abram, and Abram famously placed
his faith in the God who called him. Yet, in spite of his rela-
tive lack of knowledge about God and the daunting nature of
the challenge before him, Abram knew one thing with certainty. The change before him was great, but the promise was
far greater. Notice again Genesis 12:2–3:

> And I will make you into a great nation,
> And I will bless you,
> And make your name great;
> And you shall be a blessing;
> And I will bless those who bless you,
> And the one who curses you I will curse.
> And in you all the families of the earth will be blessed.

The scope of that promise is nothing short of staggering—
especially since, at this point, Abram and his wife, Sarai, were
childless. If it required a measure of faith to leave his family and homeland to trek to an unknown destination, how
much greater was the faith required to believe that a seventy-
five-year-old childless nomad would have the legacy of a

"great nation," a "great name," and the privilege of being the instrument through which "all the families of the earth will be blessed"?

Now, by any definition, *that* is a promise—even if it may have not felt very promising at the moment Abram received it.

Interestingly, this is a conditional promise. Sometimes, a promise in the Bible is unconditional, meaning that God will keep the promise with no action required on our part. For example, when the Lord says, "I will never leave you nor forsake you" (Hebrews 13:5 NKJV), His abiding presence is assured—no matter what we do or do not do.

A conditional promise, however, is only valid if a condition is fulfilled. For Abram, the condition was to leave his family and homeland and follow God's leading to an unknown place.

Genesis 12:4 gives us Abram's response to the condition: "So Abram went away as the LORD had spoken to him."

The condition was met, and the promise was validated. And though the promise was conditional, it was utterly trustworthy because God himself—the ultimate promise keeper—was the promise maker. Through many twists and turns, with some daring moments of faith and some dark and disappointing moments of spiritual failure along the way, the next ten chapters of Genesis tell the long story of the first evidence of the promise being fulfilled. God buttressed His promises to Abraham with the more specific promise of a son (18:10), who would be the first installment on the grand, sweeping promises of Genesis 12. The birth of Isaac (Genesis 21) to the now one-hundred-year-old Abraham by his wife, Sarah, made possible the promise of a great nation—the proverbial mighty oak growing from a single, tiny acorn.

The promise had been made, the condition was fulfilled, and the first step to fulfillment has begun. So all is well, right? A happy ending apart from any fear, danger, or threat, right? Not so much. Because the promise would be tested, and the test is as disturbing as anything we read anywhere in the Old Testament.

A Promise Tested

A film I have intentionally never seen, *Sophie's Choice*, is not necessarily one I would recommend for a variety of reasons, but it is most decisively a gut-wrenching tale that would cause any parent to cringe deeply. In post-World War II Brooklyn, Sophie eventually unpacks the dark secret of her past. When she and her two children were taken to the Auschwitz concentration camp, she was forced to choose which of her children would be spared and which would be sent to the gas chambers. Having to order the death of one of her children was a heartache she never escaped. Unable to cope with her deep guilt, Sophie in the end commits suicide.

It is an unthinkable choice. Yet, some have compared Sophie's very dark choice to the choice facing Abraham in Genesis 22:

Now it came about after these things, that God tested Abraham, and said to him, "Abraham!" And he said, "Here I am." Then He said, "Take now your son, your only son, whom you love, Isaac, and go to the land of Moriah, and offer him there as a burnt offering on one of the mountains of which I will tell you." (vv. 1–2)

As was the flood of Noah, this too is an event that troubles many in our generation. How could a loving God even ask such a thing? What good purpose could ever be accomplished by the sacrificial death of a child? *The Expositor's Bible Commentary* describes the complexities of "Abraham's inward struggle" this way:

> First, there is the abruptness of the Lord's request within the narrative. Apart from the remark in v. 1 that God's request represents a testing of Abraham, the reader has no advanced warning of the nature of the request or of its severity. Nothing in the preceding narratives has hinted at this sort of request. The reader, in other words, is as surprised as Abraham by the Lord's request. Second, the reader is given no further explanation of the request. The whole of the request is made up of three simple imperatives (v. 2): "Take" (*qaḥnā'*), "go" (*welek*), and "sacrifice him" (*weha' alēhû*). Furthermore, the reader is given no reason to believe that Abraham has any further explanation.

Like the command to leave Haran, this is yet another clear instruction from God, yet I suppose it would have been infinitely more difficult than even the hard choice to leave family and homeland to follow an invisible God to an unknown land. And this command has no promise attached to it. In fact, it is just the opposite. This command seems to threaten the ultimate fulfillment of the promise Abraham accepted in Genesis 12!

Still, promise or no promise, the thought of sacrificing your one and only child feels brutally unthinkable. *The Bible Knowledge Commentary* says:

The greatest test in the life of Abraham (God tested him) came after he received the promised seed following a long wait. The test was very real: he was to give Isaac back to God. As a test it was designed to prove faith. And for it to be a real test, it had to defy logic; it had to be something Abraham wanted to resist.

To be certain, not all of life's difficult or painful challenges are divine tests—but this one was. Nevertheless, to Abraham the choice was not merely a choice. It was a command to be obeyed.

So Abraham got up early in the morning and saddled his donkey, and took two of his young men with him and his son Isaac; and he split wood for the burnt offering, and set out and went to the place of which God had told him (Genesis 22:3)

In response to God's command in Genesis 12, we read, "So Abram went away as the LORD had spoken to him" (v. 4). Now, in Genesis 22, we read similar words, "So Abraham . . . set out and went." This is pretty remarkable. When there was a promise, Abraham obeyed. When the embodiment of that promise was threatened, Abraham still obeyed.

I don't know how that strikes you, but it hits me in two different ways. First, I am unconvinced that I would so readily obey at the cost of my child's life. Who could? Second, I am pretty sure that I would struggle to trust God to keep His promise when faced with a choice like this. And my emotional responses to this command come with the fact that I am blessed to have far more information about the heart and character of God than was available to Abraham. Wiersbe captures the test well:

Consider how unreasonable God's request was. Isaac was Abraham's only son, and the future of the covenant rested in him. Isaac was a miracle child, the gift of God to Abraham and Sarah in response to their faith. Abraham and Sarah loved Isaac very much and had built their whole future around him. When God asked Abraham to offer his son, He was testing Abraham's faith, hope, and love, and it looked like God was wiping out everything Abraham and Sarah had lived for.

Still, Abraham set out and went. And we go with him, Isaac, and the servants to the designated place for this sacrifice—a mountain. Mount Moriah. As Abraham went, he did so with a surprising level of confidence in the promise God had made so many years before—a confidence he hinted at when they arrived at Mount Moriah.

Abraham said to his young men, "Stay here with the donkey, and I and the boy will go over there; and *we will worship and return* to you." (22:5; emphasis added)

That is awesome. "*We* will worship and return."
We.
Both of us.
Together.
Abraham *and* the son of the promise.
There has been much speculation about what Abraham believed in that moment of extraordinary trust in God. Some reckon that he believed God would raise Isaac from the dead, as alluded to in Hebrews 11:19: "He considered that God is able to raise people even from the dead, from which he also

received him back as a type." What a powerful statement of confidence in the God Abraham had learned to trust!

Others propose that Abraham believed there would be a reprieve—a last-minute stay of execution—because of Genesis 22:7–8:

> Isaac spoke to his father Abraham and said, "My father!" And he said, "Here I am, my son." And he said, "Look, the fire and the wood, but where is the lamb for the burnt offering?" Abraham said, "God will provide for Himself the lamb for the burnt offering, my son." So the two of them walked on together.

This too is dramatic, and while Hebrews 11:19 seems to portray Abraham as looking forward to the exercise of God's power, I would suggest that Genesis 22:7–8 looks backward—to the promise. "God will provide" is a statement of present confidence rooted in past experience. Having spent the previous two and a half decades learning of God's trustworthiness, Abraham trusted in God's past promises during his present distress—and, in fact, God *did* provide. After commanding Abraham to restrain his knife hand rather than killing Isaac, God made the sacrifice available:

> Then Abraham raised his eyes and looked, and behold, behind him was a ram caught in the thicket by its horns; and Abraham went and took the ram and offered it up as a burnt offering in the place of his son. And Abraham named that place The LORD Will Provide, as it is said to this day, "On the mountain of the LORD it will be provided." (vv. 13–14)

The God Abraham was still getting to know had proven worthy of Abraham's trust, so Abraham gave this place a name—Jehovah Jireh, "the LORD will provide," or more literally, "the LORD will see to it." The Lord who had provided a homeland and a promise and a child had provided the sacrifice.

A place of costly sacrifice became a place of divine provision—and the promise lived on. But that isn't the end of Mount Moriah—or the story God tells there.

A Promise Extended

The location of this event is not an unimportant data point in the story. It is not a throwaway item or a piece of useless trivia. Mount Moriah becomes a pivotal location in the Bible's story. That seems to be an overly strong statement when you consider that Moriah is named only one other time in the Bible, but that other mention moves the story forward in telling ways.

Later in the Old Testament, Israel's King David sinned by numbering the people (see 2 Samuel 24 for the full account). He faced God's corrective discipline, so he sought a way to somehow limit the scope of that discipline. How could that judgment be mitigated? The prophet Gad gave David instructions: "So Gad came to David that day and said to him, 'Go up, erect an altar to the LORD on the threshing floor of Araunah the Jebusite'" (2 Samuel 24:18).

Out of deference to the king, Araunah offered the threshing floor as a gift to David as the site for the altar and its eventual sacrifices. But David refused:

However, the king said to Araunah, "No, but I will surely buy it from you for a price, for I will not offer burnt offerings to the LORD my God that cost me nothing." So David bought the threshing floor and the oxen for fifty shekels of silver. Then David built there an altar to the LORD, and he offered burnt offerings and peace offerings. And the LORD responded to prayer for the land, and the plague was withdrawn from Israel. (vv. 24–25)

The key phrase is "that cost me nothing." There was cost involved in making right what David had gotten wrong.

You may be thinking, Okay, what's the point? The point is that this event seems like an unwanted distraction unless you notice the next time Araunah's threshing floor is mentioned and identified in the biblical story.

Move ahead to the days of Solomon, David's son and the successor to Israel's throne. Solomon's desire was to fulfill David's dream of building a temple for the Lord in Jerusalem.

Where should it be built?

Then Solomon began to build the house of the LORD in Jerusalem on Mount Moriah, where the LORD had appeared to his father David, at the place that David had prepared on the threshing floor of Ornan the Jebusite. (2 Chronicles 3:1)

A place of costly sacrifice for Abraham once again became a place of costly sacrifice for David's line.

Mount Moriah became the location of Solomon's temple—which was to be "a house of prayer for all the peoples"

(Isaiah 56:7). It was a place where centuries of sacrifices were offered at great cost.

Mount Moriah had been the location of David's sacrifice—at great cost.

Mount Moriah had been the place where Abraham was expecting to sacrifice his son, Isaac.

Mount Moriah became a place in the Old Testament consistently identified with costly sacrifice. This reality of costly sacrifice takes the promise God made to Abraham and the test that the promise underwent and turns them into a picture—a picture of how that promise would ultimately, finally, and eternally be fulfilled.

Think back again to the promise God gave in Genesis 12. How would all the families of the earth be blessed through Abraham's seed?

Not through the temple.

Not through the sacrifices of countless lambs.

In John 2, Jesus strode into the temple in Jerusalem—Herod's temple, located on the temple mount, that is, the ancient Mount Moriah—and began to cleanse it of the thievery and misrepresentation of God that had taken over the house of God. When the Jewish leaders asked Jesus what gave Him the authority for such a daring and dramatic act, He responded:

> "Destroy this temple, and in three days I will raise it up." The Jews then said, "It took forty-six years to build this temple, and yet You will raise it up in three days?" But He was speaking about the temple of His body. So when He was raised from the dead, His disciples remembered that He said this; and they believed

the Scripture and the word which Jesus had spoken. (vv. 19–22).

All the families of the earth would be blessed through a new and better temple—the body of Jesus. God's one and only Son. But in the case of Jesus, Jehovah Jireh did not provide a lamb to rescue His Son. Instead, God provided His Son as the Lamb who came to our rescue! In that sacrifice, God's ancient promise to Abram was fulfilled, and quite literally all the nations of the earth have been blessed as God's saving love has redeemed men and women "from every tribe, language, people, and nation" (Revelation 5:9).

God provided His Son as the Lamb who came to our rescue!

Jesus provided the greatest sacrifice at the greatest cost to reveal something beyond anything we could have ever imagined—expressing God's promise with beauty and grace: "But God demonstrates His own love toward us, in that while we were still sinners, Christ died for us" (Romans 5:8).

It has been said that the measure of love is what you are willing to give up for it. Abraham's story of the costly near sacrifice of a beloved son set the stage for love's most extravagant display—the sacrifice of Jesus, who laid down His life to rescue us from our sins and set us free. It's the picture of Mount Moriah fulfilled and the love of God lavishly displayed. As Isaac Watts wrote:

Was it for crimes that I had done
He groaned upon the tree?
Amazing pity! grace unknown!
And love beyond degree!

At the cross, at the cross where I first saw the light,
And the burden of my heart rolled away,
It was there by faith I received my sight,
And now I am happy all the day!

3

The Law Is Given

In recent years, I have grown to love the Western novels of Louis L'Amour. Tales of the American West have long fascinated me, but L'Amour's stories opened up new windows of understanding for me. Though writing fiction, L'Amour was a careful historian. He researched locations, validated his ideas through conversations with people who were eyewitnesses of those times, and added things he had learned from his own experiences growing up in Jamestown, North Dakota—where cowboys and cattle were still a common sight in the early twentieth century. All those elements combined with L'Amour's expansive talent as a storyteller to create some of the most enduring characters in Western fiction—Hondo Lane, the Sacketts, Conagher, and Kilkenny to name just a few. His eighty-nine novels and fourteen collections of short stories continue to be loved and enjoyed by millions.

In those stories, there is a consistent—even systemic—characteristic of the Old West. It was, for the most part, a lawless place. For most of the nineteenth century, law was determined by whoever had the power, and justice was meted out with a gun. For this reason, famous lawmen of the West— men like Wyatt Earp, Bat Masterson, Wild Bill Hickok, and Pat Garrett—became almost mythic characters who loomed large over the towns where they sought to tame the lawlessness of the territory and make it a place where families could safely be raised. That safety required law and people who were strong enough to enforce it.

Despite the veneer of sophistication that covers modern culture, in many ways, not much has changed. A lawlessness runs just under the surface of our hearts—part of our human brokenness—and it needs restraining. Because some people will not restrain themselves, laws and law enforcement officers must act as a restraining presence to maintain a peaceful, orderly society.

Law matters. And laws matter.

Today, the thin thread of civilization, on a human level at least, is held intact by these laws that our societies have agreed upon in conjunction with the fair and just administration of those laws. To be fair, it is far from an easy task, for the more complex a society becomes, the more difficult it is to provide fair play for all. But today, as it was in the American West, law is a vitally important part of a healthy society.

So, from our current day we travel back through the days of the Wild, Wild West all the way to ancient times, for Israel also had a set of laws. And although the long centuries taught them the difficulties of keeping the law, they learned the importance of law as well—and they began that learning process at the base of a mountain.

A Journey to Freedom

The backstory to this tale of law is one of the most important in the Old Testament, involving a number of players in the unfolding drama. Jacob (the son of Isaac, Abraham's son of the promise seen in chapter 2) and his family, which was truly dysfunctional, were living in Canaan, the land God promised to Abraham. A destructive sibling rivalry between Joseph, Jacob's son, and his brothers erupted into violence (Genesis 37), resulting in Joseph being sold into slavery by his own brothers. Joseph was trafficked from Canaan to Egypt, but over the course of the next thirteen years, Joseph climbed to a position of leadership in Egypt that was second only to Pharaoh (Genesis 41). Then, following seven years of abundance, seven years of famine began. Joseph's brothers joined the throngs traveling from around the known world to visit Egypt to buy food. After a difficult reunion with his brothers (Genesis 45), Joseph used his authority in Egypt to invite his family—some seventy persons in number—to reside in his new homeland so he could provide for them.

More than four hundred years transpired, and during that time, the children of Israel (another name for Jacob) grew into a massive number of people, creating what the new Pharaoh considered an internal security threat (Exodus 1). As a result, he subjected the Hebrew people to slavery, even going so far as to commit infanticide by demanding that all male Hebrew babies be killed at birth. Into this dark and difficult environment, Moses was born, and through a series of circumstances (Exodus 2) found himself far from Egypt. While Moses lived in Midian, God called him to be His agent for delivering the children of Israel from bondage in Egypt and leading them into a land of promise.

So, after the Israelites spent more than four centuries in Egypt—much of the time in slavery—God sent the promised deliverer. Through a variety of supernatural events (the ten plagues), God rescued His chosen people from bondage. After passing through the Red Sea to safety, the people exhibited a mixture of celebration and irritation. They celebrated God's dynamic act of rescue on their behalf as the waters of the Red Sea parted and the Hebrews passed through on dry land (Exodus 15). However, when just a few days later they lacked water and food, they accused Moses of bringing them into the wilderness to die. This pattern of rescue followed by celebration followed by murmuring and complaining would mark the experience of the children of Israel over the coming forty years in the wilderness.

After a miraculous provision of food and water (Exodus 16–17), the Hebrews finally reached their first real stopping point in their exodus—and it was at the foot of a mountain:

> In the third month after the sons of Israel had gone out of the land of Egypt, on that very day they came into the wilderness of Sinai. When they set out from Rephidim, they came to the wilderness of Sinai and camped in the wilderness; and there Israel camped in front of the mountain. (19:1–2)

That's a lot of backstory, but we are now where we need to be—at Mount Sinai. Imagine if you will the spectacle at the base of Sinai. *The Bible Knowledge Commentary* helps us to get a sense of the scope of the scene:

> The number of Israelite men was about 600,000 (in 38:26 and Numbers 1:46 the exact figure is 603,550).

With women and children, the number of Israelites was about 2 million. With them were non-Israelites of an undesignated number, apparently a variegated group (a "rabble," Numbers 11:4). In the wilderness they caused the Israelites to complain against Moses.

Some scholars estimate the number of the Hebrews as much less, but even the lowest estimates (around fifty thousand total) reveal a massive crowd that had to be cared for, led, and governed. It was for this cause that the people of Israel arrived at Sinai. It was here that governance would begin—and it would begin with the giving of the law.

The Birth of the Israelite Nation

Most Americans can easily identify the events of the date July 4, 1776. With the signing of the Declaration of Independence, the thirteen English colonies in the New World declared their determination to be self-governing. Of course, this declaration launched the Revolutionary War, which ended on September 3, 1783, when British General Lord Charles Cornwallis surrendered to the colonials at Yorktown, Virginia.

However, that long, bloody war did not ensure the establishment of a nation—it only secured the opportunity for the colonies to build a nation. That nation needed laws, and those laws were not actually endorsed until 1788! It took almost as long to develop the system of laws that would govern the American nation as it took to complete the war to secure their freedom.

That fledgling American nation actually had a lot in common with the children of Israel at the foot of Sinai. Having gained their freedom, they needed a national identity, a central government, and a set of laws.

All of that would be resolved at Mount Sinai—and more. Remember, for some four hundred years, the children of Abraham, Isaac, and Jacob not only had been in Egypt but had also been separated from their God. God had reintroduced himself to the Israelites through the signs and wonders that had catalyzed their release from slavery. Now they would come to meet Him more personally and begin to understand the unique calling and role that awaited them. That's why rehearsing the history of Israel from Abraham to Moses matters so much. As theologian Richard Hays says in *Reading with the Grain of Scripture*:

> There is no such thing as a law that has normative force and validity outside of a particular cultural system, or— to put the point in a more biblical fashion—outside of a particular story. The biblical account of the origin of Torah makes this point very clear. The Law is derived neither by some sort of democratic process nor by reason's unaided contemplation of the night sky; rather, the Law is given by God to a people he has graciously chosen, rescued from slavery in Egypt, and led to the foot of Mount Sinai, where he summons his servant Moses to receive a revelatory disclosure of God's order and God's will. . . . The laws given to Moses have binding force because they are the decrees of a Lawgiver who is first of all creator and savior of the people to whom they are given.

As a result, it was at Sinai that several important things happened as the people encountered the God of their fathers.

First, as we have seen, God formally reintroduced himself to His chosen people:

> The LORD also said to Moses, "Go to the people and consecrate them today and tomorrow, and have them wash their garments; and have them ready for the third day, for on the third day *the Lord will come down on Mount Sinai* in the sight of all the people. (Exodus 19:10–11; emphasis added)

During their time in Egypt, it seems clear that many—perhaps even most—of the children of Israel had shifted their allegiance from the God of their ancestors to the gods of Egypt. This condition of distance from God is borne out later at Mount Sinai when, during a lengthy absence by Moses, the people demand that Aaron give them a golden calf to worship (Exodus 32)—accrediting their rescue from Egypt to that false idol! This apparently widespread acceptance of idolatry was not only foolish but also in direct violation of the first laws God established for them—the Ten Commandments—as we see in Exodus 20:3–6,

> You shall have no other gods before Me.
> You shall not make for yourself an idol, or any likeness of what is in heaven above or on the earth beneath, or in the water under the earth. You shall not worship them nor serve them; for I, the LORD your God, am a jealous God, inflicting the punishment of the fathers on the children, on the third and the fourth generations of those who hate Me, but showing favor to thousands, to those who love Me and keep My commandments.

The ease with which Israel slid back into idolatry may reveal just how far they had drifted from their God, and it was at Sinai that Israel experienced the God who had called and chosen them to be His own. This introduction resulted in the very thing that came to most singularly identify Israel—their unique relationship to the one true God in a world filled with idolatry and polytheism.

Second, at Sinai Israel morphed from an enormous extended family into an actual nation, with the law of Moses being the constitution of that nation. This is important because, as we can now see, these people were fulfilling God's promise to Abraham that a great nation would come from his offspring. Whereas the children of Israel had arrived at Sinai as a mob of loosely connected family units without a unifying identity, they leave Mount Sinai as a national entity. In fact, they leave Sinai as a theocracy—a monarchy in which God himself ruled as king.

At Sinai Israel entered into a covenant with God in which He agreed to be their God and they agreed to be His people. A covenant, in modern terms, is a formal, legally binding agreement. We may be most familiar with the term being used at weddings to describe the marriage covenant. Two parties agree to live together as husband and wife—and they seal that covenant with vows and promises.

At Sinai, God promised to be Israel's God and to care for them, provide a homeland for them, and watch over them. In return, the people agreed to obey the laws that God established for them:

Then Moses came and reported to the people all the words of the LORD and all the ordinances; and all the people answered with one voice and said, "All the words which the LORD has spoken we will do!" (Exodus 24:3)

The establishment of these laws, however, included more than just public regulations—the necessary guidelines required for an orderly society. It also included religious ordinances to guide them as the chosen people in the worship and celebration of the one true God. Both of those purposes—civil and ceremonial—carried a larger purpose. These people, who had spent four centuries in a strange land dominated by polytheistic religion, were challenged to a new way. A better way.

As such, on a practical level, the law was a teaching device, intended to teach the once *children* of Israel and now *nation* of Israel to choose God's way over any and every other way, and the law was also intended to be a continual reminder that apart from God's help real obedience to that law was impossible. Their covenant agreement in Exodus 24:3 was their voiced commitment to choose this better way to which God had called and chosen them.

> The law was a teaching device, intended to teach . . . Israel to choose God's way over any and every other way.

So, at the base of Mount Sinai, we witness the birth of the Israelite nation—and that nation's covenant agreement to live as a people of God. None of this was superfluous or unnecessary. The God of their fathers was leading these people to a land where they would be an island of monotheism in the midst of an ocean of idolatry. To solidify their relationship with God was both preparation for and protection against the spiritual threats that awaited them in the land of promise.

God gave them national structure.

God gave them national laws.

God gave them a national faith.

God gave them himself.

Sinai was the place where all these transformational events occurred, and while the road ahead was far from smooth—there were, after all, forty years of wilderness wanderings ahead—the now nation of Israel would stride forward in the presence of their God.

From slavery in Egypt to chosen people of God. Everything had changed for Israel—and it happened at the mountain.

The Larger Reality

So, it's all good, right? No. As we saw, one golden calf later, the covenant was already broken. Why? Because, in spite of the people's commitment—no doubt well intended—to obey the law, they were incapable of doing so. This has ever and always been the problem with the law. It cannot bring us back to God; indeed that was never its intended purpose.

This new Israelite nation genuinely meant it when they said they would obey—but they never could keep that promise in their own energy, which Simon Peter acknowledged in Acts 15:10. There, he explained to Jewish believers why the law should be nonbinding on gentile followers of Christ:

Since this is the case, why are you putting God to the test by placing upon the neck of the disciples a yoke which neither our forefathers nor we have been able to bear?

And yet, even if we were able to bear the law, it was never intended to be the path back to God. In his first recorded message in the book of Acts, Paul preached the death and resurrection of Jesus as the one and only way to God, precisely because the law could *not* set us free!

Therefore let it be known to you, brothers, that through Him forgiveness of sins is proclaimed to you, and through Him everyone who believes is freed from all things, from which you could not be freed through the Law of Moses. (Acts 13:38–39)

Obedience to the law is just as much beyond our grasp as it was beyond theirs. So, what was the point of the law? Again, to give us a place where we learn our deep need of Him, His wisdom, and ultimately His grace. And this puts us on track with the big story of the Bible—which is the story of Jesus. Reflect once more on a verse we saw in an earlier chapter:

For the Law was given through Moses; grace and truth were realized through Jesus Christ. (John 1:17)

As grace and truth came through Jesus, He also set about to do what we could not do: He kept the law on our behalf. In His first major address recorded in Matthew's gospel— the Sermon on the Mount—Jesus confirmed this aspect of His mission:

Do not presume that I came to abolish the Law or the Prophets; I did not come to abolish, but to fulfill. (Matthew 5:17)

He came to fulfill the law on our behalf because we were never going to be able to accomplish that feat. Mount Sinai portrays the mountain of law—revealing to us our inadequacy and our great need of Jesus. So, since we could never fulfill the law, the Christ who perfectly fulfilled the law provided rescue for us from the law's curse:

But when the fullness of the time came, God sent His Son, born of a woman, born under the Law, so that He might redeem those who were under the Law, that we might receive the adoption as sons and daughters. (Galatians 4:4–5)

In a sense, this is Paul's theological telling of the Christmas story. One of the underappreciated aspects of Jesus's mission was that He came not only to save us from our sins (Matthew 1:21) but also to redeem those who were under the law of Sinai, which could never be our path to God. To *redeem*

Mount Sinai portrays the mountain of law—revealing to us our inadequacy and our great need of Jesus.

was a term used to describe buying someone from the slave market to set that person free—just as God did with Israel's rescue from Egypt. But our redemption is not the result of Moses's law. It is the result of Jesus's death and resurrection.

Thomas O. Chisholm, the hymn writer who gave us the classic hymn "Great Is Thy Faithfulness," also wrote about the redemption that our faithful God has given us from the curse of the law—reminding us both of Israel's experience and our deliverance:

> I well remember when I saw
> Myself condemned before the law,
> Heard Sinai's awful thunders roll,
> While fear possessed my trembling soul.
>
> "Not under law," that could not save,
> But doomed me to a hopeless grave;
> "But under grace," where I am free
> Through Jesus Christ who died for me.

4

Choices and Consequences

I had just finished teaching the first of four sessions for the Our Daily Bread Bible Conference in Jakarta, Indonesia, when during a break the team surprised me by playing a special video. As it turned out, this was my fifteenth Bible conference in Jakarta, and the staff had put together this video to celebrate that landmark moment. Like everything our Jakarta team does, the presentation was gracious and first-class, but the stunning moment came when a clip played from our very first conference together. My hair had been considerably darker then, but, lo and behold, at that first conference I was wearing the same blue batik shirt I was wearing for the fifteenth conference as well. It had been given to me for that first conference and, thankfully, it still fit. But the laughter really came when on the fifteen-year-old video clip, I made the exact same statement I had just said in the fifteenth conference! The conferences focused on the stories of two different Bible characters, but the comment about application was the same.

Choices have consequences.

When the second session began, we laughed together about the "learning by repetition" moment we just had by way of the video—but in that moment I realized that in almost every story of almost every person in the Bible, that startling reality holds true.

Choices have consequences.

I have experienced that in my own life as well, and I'm sure you have too. When I was in tenth grade, I came home from school and dropped my books inside the door, turning to leave immediately. My mom stopped me and asked where I was going. When I told her I was going to a friend's house to play football, she informed me that I wasn't going anywhere until I did my homework. So, as a good, obedient son, I snuck out the back door and went to play football. All went well until, on the final play of the game, I was tackled into a swing set—breaking one of my front teeth.

I slunk home knowing I couldn't hide what had happened, and without question there would be immediate consequences to my choice to play football—consequences that were enforced as soon as my dad got home from work. That wasn't the end of it, however. That broken tooth led to a series of dental issues that, over the next twenty-five years, resulted in thousands of dollars in expenses. In fact, I'm pretty sure I put a couple of dentists' kids through college. Thousands of dollars and twenty-five years—stretching even into my current dental experiences today.

Choices have consequences.

Or as Roy Hobbs put it in the baseball movie *The Natural,* "Some mistakes you never stop paying for."

Understand that my choice to sneak out and play football was not a moment of abject rebellion or angry determination. It was one seemingly insignificant choice in a random moment that produced consequences I have had to live with for the rest of my life.

Did I mention that choices have consequences?

As we return to our consideration of important biblical events on important biblical mountains, we arrive at what I suspect is the most obscure of the mountains we will consider together. After all, not many of us have ever heard a sermon series on Mount Nebo—but that mountain was the place where Moses faced the consequences of one of his choices.

An Important Context

Every Bible college and seminary around the world that takes the Bible seriously offers hermeneutics. Hermeneutics is, as one of my profs put it, the science and art of interpreting the Scriptures. After all, understanding what the Bible says is only helpful to the extent that we understand what the Bible *means* by what it says. This is the job of hermeneutics: seeking to understand the Spirit-inspired meaning and message of any particular biblical text.

In every one of those classes, it is drilled into the heads and hearts of the students that, among the many helpful factors that give us insight into the Scriptures, no single factor aids our understanding more than the context of the text. Getting the context straight forces us to ask important questions:

What Testament is it in?

What book is it in?

Who is speaking or writing?

To whom is the writer writing or speaking?

What is in the verses just before and just after the text?

All those ideas help to form the context. The word *context* comes from two Latin words that combine to mean "to weave together"—and that is exactly what we are talking about: weaving together the verse and its textual surroundings to assure the most accurate understanding possible. That is important perspective as we approach Deuteronomy 32:49, which brings us to God's command to Moses to ascend Mount Nebo.

> Go up to this mountain of the Abarim, Mount Nebo, which is in the land of Moab opposite Jericho, and look at the land of Canaan, which I am giving to the sons of Israel as a possession.

So, now that we've made our way to Mount Nebo, what is the context for this verse?

We are clearly in the Old Testament and obviously in the book of Deuteronomy. The word *Deuteronomy* means "second law," which gives us the important reason for this final entry of the five books of Moses (the Torah or Pentateuch). We saw in chapter three that at Mount Sinai, Israel became a nation and entered into a covenant agreement with the God of their forefathers—which involved a commitment to keep the laws of Moses.

However, forty years had transpired since Israel left Sinai. The generation that had agreed to be God's covenant people had passed away in the wilderness. Now a new generation was preparing to enter the land God had promised to them—and part of that preparation involved this new generation being reminded of what their parents had committed them to be. A people of God.

As a result, Moses rehearsed the law of Mount Sinai to the people as they neared the Jordan River, in order to renew the people's commitment to their covenant relationship with God. And that teaching and reinforcing of the law basically consumed the first thirty-one-plus chapters of Deuteronomy.

Which brings us to Mount Nebo.

The *Lexham Bible Dictionary* provides us with this information about Nebo:

> Mount Nebo figures prominently in the books of Numbers and Deuteronomy. . . . Numbers 33:47 identifies this mountain as Nebo. Deuteronomy 32:49 repeats this account. Deuteronomy 34:1 indicates that Nebo is located at the plains of Moab, across from Jericho. The same verse also equates Nebo with Pisgah (which would locate Nebo within the territory of Reuben, east of the Jordan River; see Josh 13:20). Numbers 21:20 seems to support this location, as it states that Pisgah was in the valley of the land of Moab.

This location is important for a couple of reasons. First, Mount Nebo is the place from which the children of Israel (and Moses) get their first glimpse of the promised land. Remember, they had spent the last forty years in wilderness wanderings, sustained miraculously by manna, quail, and water provided by their covenant God.

Think about the harsh conditions they had endured. Think of the weariness of those four decades, as the people must have wondered as they wandered, Will we ever get there? What will this new homeland be like? God had promised them a "land flowing with milk and honey" (Exodus 3:8). Would their new home live up to those expectations?

It is at Mount Nebo that they began to get answers to those very important questions—and it is also the mountain where another very important thing happened. While the command to ascend Mount Nebo and look on the land was preparation for the people corporately, this second event would happen to Moses personally. With the context firmly in place, see what God told Moses next:

> Then you are to die on the mountain where you ascend, and be gathered to your people, as Aaron your brother died on Mount Hor and was gathered to his people, because you broke faith with Me in the midst of the sons of Israel at the waters of Meribah-kadesh, in the wilderness of Zin, because you did not treat Me as holy in the midst of the sons of Israel. For you will see the land at a distance but you will not go there, into the land which I am giving the sons of Israel." (Deuteronomy 32:50–52)

The Lord spoke to Moses, now 120 years of age, and said that it would be there—at Mount Nebo—that Israel's great leader would face the consequences of a choice he had made years before, during the days of wilderness wandering. First, we must consider the choice, then we will grapple with the consequences.

An Insignificant Choice

The website AnswersToAll says:

We make dozens of decisions every day, some simple, some more complex. Some internet sources estimate that an adult makes about 35,000 conscious decisions each day. We make 226.7 decisions each day on just food alone according to researchers at Cornell University.

The *Daily Mirror*, a newspaper in the United Kingdom, offers much more modest but surprisingly precise numbers: "The average person will make 773,618 decisions over a lifetime—and will come to regret 143,262 of them."

I don't know about you, but to me that feels pretty overwhelming. In fact, statistics like those could easily become paralyzing. Especially as we consider the idea that all those thousands and thousands of choices have consequences! Those choices come in all shapes and sizes, and they are certainly not all created equal. Yet, choices are part of the free will God has given to us—and that freedom is not to be exercised indiscriminately, for, when we make unwise choices, those choices can have disproportionate consequences (like my lifetime of dental adventures). Which brings us back to Moses and his choice.

God referenced the choice in question in Deuteronomy 32:51:

. . . because you broke faith with Me in the midst of the sons of Israel at the waters of Meribah-kadesh, in the wilderness of Zin, because you did not treat Me as holy in the midst of the sons of Israel.

To find this event, we have to travel back to Numbers 20. As we drop down into the fourth book of Moses, we start again with the context. In the opening verses of Numbers 20, Miriam (Moses's sister) died and was buried. It was in this season of loss that Moses faced (again) the challenges of leading the children of Israel. Israel is described five times in Deuteronomy alone as "rebellious" and seven times in Exodus and Deuteronomy as "stiff-necked" (KJV). This was no easy group to lead, and the harsh conditions of the wilderness through which they were traveling continually exacerbated Moses's challenging mission of leadership.

In Numbers 20, this explosive concoction went off—and Moses added in his own problems. Throughout the biblical record, Moses has displayed some serious anger-management issues (see Exodus 11:8, 16:20, 32:19; Leviticus 10:16; Numbers 16:15, 31:14), and the grumbling of the people (perhaps felt even more harshly in Moses's season of grief over the death of his sister) triggered his anger once more. As the people complained yet again about their lack of water, the Lord gave clear instructions to Moses:

> Take the staff; and you and your brother Aaron assemble the congregation and speak to the rock before their eyes, that it shall yield its water. So you shall bring water for them out of the rock, and have the congregation and their livestock drink. (Numbers 20:8)

Speak to the rock.

Earlier in their journey, God had instructed Moses to strike a rock to provide water for the people (Exodus 17:6). Here, however, the instructions were different. Moses was not to *strike* the rock; rather, he was to *speak* to the rock—which,

Paul later asserted, represented Jesus himself (1 Corinthians 10:4)! Moses, however, responded out of his anger and frustration. He chose to ignore God's instructions and vented his anger by using a different means to get water from the rock:

> So Moses took the staff from before the LORD, just as He had commanded him; and Moses and Aaron summoned the assembly in front of the rock. And he said to them, "Listen now, you rebels; shall we bring water for you out of this rock?" Then Moses raised his hand and struck the rock twice with his staff; and water came out abundantly, and the congregation and their livestock drank. (Numbers 20:9–11)

The two notable things seen here are that, first, Moses verbalized his frustrations with the people ("you rebels") and then acted on them with the rock ("struck the rock twice"). Still, after this brief exchange, water flowed freely from the rock, the people and livestock were satisfied, and all was well. Right?

Not exactly.

Moses had taken matters, quite literally, into his own hands and ignored God's instructions. Inherent in that act, however, was something more subtle. Something riding just under the surface, yet fueling Moses's anger. Notice again Moses's words:

> Listen now, you rebels; *shall we bring* water for you out of this rock? (v. 10; emphasis added)

Perhaps the most important component to the entire event is the little word *we*. Rather than directing the people's attention (yet again) to the Lord as their source and sustainer, Moses assumed that role for himself and Aaron. Long gone were the days of his understanding and acceptance of his own inadequacy (Exodus 3:11; 4:10), now replaced by the bravado to claim that *he* was their provider and rescuer. It was Moses who was in charge. *The Expositor's Bible Commentary* unpacks this crucial moment in this way:

> Even the rash words of Moses were an act of rebellion against the Spirit of God. This is the conclusion of the poet in Psalm 106:32–33; he rehearses these events in song:

> By the waters of Meribah they angered the LORD,
> and trouble came to Moses because of them;
> for they rebelled against the Spirit of God,
> and rash words came from Moses' lips.

Rash words. Presumptive words. And, in the end, words by which Moses claimed the glory of this provision for himself (and Aaron) rather than directing the honor and thanks to God, the true provider. *The Expositor's Bible Commentary* expands this further:

> The text specifies two reasons for this painful reality. In the first place, Moses "broke faith" with Yahweh. This verb signifies a breach of a relationship of trust between persons or with God (Wakely, *NIDOTTE*, 2:1020). The covenantal mediator's conduct at Meribah represented disloyalty. That whole episode was regarded as an act of rebellion throughout Israelite history (Numbers 20:24; cf. 27:14; 1 Samuel 12:15). Second, Moses

failed to "uphold holiness." His actions at Meribah did not demonstrate a proper recognition of Yahweh's absolute sovereignty and uniqueness. In spite of this offense, Yahweh will allow Moses the privilege of viewing the long-anticipated land before he dies.

Over the years, many have argued that this wasn't such a big deal. He struck rather than speaking. So what? Clearly, Moses was at his wit's end and the people had worn down whatever remaining shreds of patience he had. A bit of a snap of temper is understandable, right?

From a human perspective, perhaps.

From God's perspective, not at all.

> **Because Moses robbed God of His honor, there were consequences.**

That is the reasoning behind God's discipline of His chosen leader for His chosen people:

> But the LORD said to Moses and Aaron, "Since you did not trust in Me, to treat Me as holy in the sight of the sons of Israel, for that reason you shall not bring this assembly into the land which I have given them." Those were called the waters of Meribah, because the sons of Israel argued with the LORD, and He proved Himself holy among them. (Numbers 20:12–13)

Because Moses robbed God of His honor, there were consequences—Moses would see the land of promise, which had been their destination for some forty years, but he would not be allowed to lead the people into it. Which brings us back to Mount Nebo.

An Instructive Consequence

Some say that Moses's punishment doesn't fit his crime. That God was overly harsh. Yet, we must understand this consequence in the context of the entire exodus event. The giving of the law at Sinai and the Israelites' subsequent wanderings in the wilderness were prefaced with the words the Lord used to introduce the Ten Commandments:

> I am the LORD your God, who brought you out of the land of Egypt, out of the house of slavery. (Exodus 20:2)

They were to learn, first and foremost, to look to their God for everything because, as He had been their rescuer, He would be their sustainer. When Moses claimed responsibility for the provision of the water, he usurped that role. And the consequences were severe indeed.

He could see the promised land.

He could not enter the promised land.

This, by the way, was not the first time Moses reaped difficult consequences for an unwise choice. In Exodus 2, he took it into his own hands to deliver Israel from bondage by killing an Egyptian taskmaster (see Acts 7:25). That rash choice caused him to flee from Egypt to the mountains of Midian where he spent forty years learning lessons of dependence.

Now, it was the rash choice to strike the rock that cost Moses. As he had been forced to leave his home in Egypt in Exodus 2, he was now refused entrance to his promised home.

He would die and be buried on Mount Nebo—a sad end to the mostly brilliant life of Israel's greatest leader in the Old Testament era. *The New Bible Commentary* tells us:

> The Lord told him to ascend Mt Nebo, from where he would have a panoramic view, heart-rending for him, of the land which had been the purpose of his whole life, but on which he would not set foot.

There, on Mount Nebo, Moses died with his task unfinished, due to a seemingly insignificant choice years earlier.

Choices have consequences. And sometimes the cost of those consequences is very, very high. One of life's abiding realities is that we tend to live life in the flow of the moment. We don't usually stop to think about those thousands of decisions we make every day. Likewise, we don't always stop to think about what the consequences of those choices might be. But when we pause, think, pray, and consider the Scriptures, we find in our loving God the help and direction we need most in that moment.

Something to Think About

Ernest Hemingway wrote, "All stories, if continued far enough, end in death." If that is true, then Moses's story ended on Mount Nebo with an unmarked grave and a record of final failure. But, for the child of God, our stories do not end in death. Nor did Moses's story. Even in our moments of failure when our foolish, rash, or sinful choices haunt us with consequences we could have never imagined, our loving Father remains the God of mercy and grace.

Yes, Moses was prohibited from entering the land with the people he had led for those many long years.

But.

God's grace is surprising. His mercy is unending. And Moses eventually *did* enter the promised land. His entrance into the land took place at the transfiguration of Jesus. There, with three of Jesus's disciples as witnesses, Luke says this:

And behold, two men were talking with Him; and they were Moses and Elijah, who, appearing in glory, were speaking of His departure, which He was about to accomplish at Jerusalem. (9:30–31)

God is the God of all mercy. Even when we need God's discipline and chastening, even when we receive the consequences of our choices, even when we feel cut off and forsaken—God is the God of all mercy, and seeing Moses on the Mount of Transfiguration with Jesus (and Elijah) thrills me to no end. Because there (as we will explore more fully later) Jesus talked with him about what the coming events in

> Even when we receive the consequences of our choices . . . God is the God of all mercy.

Jerusalem were going to accomplish. Jesus's crucifixion, resurrection, and departure (the Greek word *exodus!*) were going to provide the sacrifice and the satisfaction not only for all of Moses's sinful choices but for ours as well, as Jesus himself bore our sins in His body on the cross (1 Peter 2:24).

Ultimately, while we may face the consequences of our choices in the here and now, Jesus took the eternal realities of those consequences on himself—so we could be set free. In the meantime, between the now and the eternal, I know that I desperately need the wisdom of God to make better choices so that I might please and honor my Savior.

My favorite hymn is "Be Thou My Vision," an ancient hymn in the Celtic tradition. Although all of the verses are thought-provoking and awe-inspiring, one in particular speaks to our need for wisdom as we make the thousands of choices that confront us every day. In fact, we need even more. We do not simply need wisdom, nor do we simply need the wisdom of God. What we need most, as Moses and the Israelites needed in the wilderness, is the God of wisdom himself. That is why this hymn teaches us to pray:

> Be thou my wisdom, and thou my true word
> I ever with thee and thou with me, Lord
> Thou my great Father, and I thy true son
> Thou in me dwelling and I with thee one.

5

M O U N T   Z I O N

A Home for the King

"There's no place like home. There's no place like home. There's no place like home."

This mantra, with the added action of clicking the heels of the ruby slippers, was all it took to magically transport Dorothy and Toto from the technicolor land of Oz back to their black-and-white home in Kansas. Unfortunately, there aren't enough ruby slippers to go around. Although many of us share Dorothy's longing for home, finding that home and securing it is sometimes easier said than done.

One of the by-products of living in a highly mobile, extremely transient society is a sense of detachment—a feeling of not belonging where you are and wondering if you will ever find that place where you truly do belong. This feeling may also reflect a deeper reality, one spoken of by C. S. Lewis in *Mere Christianity*:

> If I find in myself a desire which no experience in this world can satisfy, the most probable explanation is that I was made for another world.

This disconnect from place—whether rooted in our eternal longings or stamped by the instability of our age—is a very real, and sometimes very emotional, struggle that people face, even when their reasons for moving were good and legitimate.

In fact, this desire reaches back nearly to the beginning of human history. As we have seen, Abram and Sarai left the home they remembered for a home that God had promised, but that they quite simply could never have imagined. The children of Israel wandered for forty long years in the wilderness wondering if they would ever reach the home God had promised them. Even Jesus expressed His own lack of an earthly home, saying, "The foxes have holes and the birds of the sky have nests, but the Son of Man has nowhere to lay His head" (Matthew 8:20). And on the night before He died, Jesus explained to His disciples about His return to His Father's house (John 14:1–4).

We all long for a place called home.

And that was true of King David as well.

A Life Disconnected

A man sentenced to die for a crime he didn't commit. An escape from the authorities. A life on the run, fueled by the burning desire to prove his innocence. Yes, for those old enough to remember, that was the basic story line of the 1960s television series *The Fugitive* (a story and character revived in the 1990s in film by Harrison Ford). David Janssen played the role of Dr. Richard Kimble, the fugitive, who was tried and convicted of the murder of his wife. His wanderings, travails, and adventures, while in pursuit of the notorious one-armed man that Kimble believed to be the true killer, was good for four years and 120 episodes of quality television. And stardom for David Janssen.

Yet, what David Janssen portrayed in the make-believe world of television, David of Bethlehem experienced in real life. King David is one of Scripture's most complex and intriguing figures. He was a warrior yet a poet, a womanizer while a worship musician, a shepherd but still a king, and a villain who at times was a hero.

What was his backstory?

Anointed as king of Israel while still a youth (perhaps in his mid-teens)

Won victory over the giant Goliath

Hunted and hounded by jealous King Saul

Lived the life of a vagabond for years

Along the way, David's life was marked by moral failure, bloody conquests, deep depression, musical lament, and seasons of perceived distance from God punctuated by moments of high worship.

Did I mention that David is a complex figure?

It is during his years as a fugitive that we enter David's story. During that time, he lived as a hunted man in caves and forests and on mountains, which means that David fully understood what it meant to be homeless.

That experience of homelessness formed the core material for some of David's most profound psalms—Psalms 18, 34, 52, 54, 56, 57, 59, 63, and 142 among them. Two of these psalms (57 and 142) are particularly poignant, for there we glimpse inside the heart and mind of this man who became king—and both psalms seem to be rooted in the same biblical event. We find it in 1 Samuel 24:1–3:

> Now when Saul returned from pursuing the Philistines, it was reported to him, saying, "Behold, David is in the wilderness of Engedi." Then Saul took three thousand chosen men from all Israel and went to search for David and his men in front of the Rocks of the Mountain Goats. And he came to the sheepfolds on the way, where there was a cave; and Saul went in to relieve himself. Now David and his men were sitting in the inner recesses of the cave.

David and his men were hiding in a cave. Imagine what must have gone through his mind. So many years had passed since he had been anointed as king by the prophet Samuel in his hometown village of Bethlehem. So many close calls and daring escapes. The crown and the throne must have seemed a million miles away—if they were real at all. Now, with three thousand choice men, Saul had closed in on David.

Then Saul entered the very cave in which David and his men were hiding, ironically, to "relieve himself" (v. 3). Immediately, David's men saw the presence of Saul as a gift from God. After all the running and deprivation and despair, the enemy was at hand. Unprotected. Vulnerable. But David did not respond to that moment with relief or revenge. He responded with heartache.

Notice how he described his feelings in the lament of Psalm 142:1–4:

> I cry out with my voice to the LORD;
> With my voice I implore the LORD for compassion.
> I pour out my complaint before Him;
> I declare my trouble before Him.
> When my spirit felt weak within me,
> You knew my path.
> In the way where I walk
> They have hidden a trap for me.
> Look to the right and see;
> For there is no one who regards me favorably;
> There is no escape for me;
> No one cares for my soul.

Every time I read that last line, I get a lump in my throat. *No one cares for my soul.*

It is a feeling that most (if not all) of us experience at one time or another. A feeling of the darkest kind of despair. A feeling of having been abandoned by one and all. It is a hard

> Homeless and hiding, haunted and hunted, David understood what it meant to feel rootless.

place to be—and an even harder way to live. Homeless and hiding, haunted and hunted, David understood what it meant to feel rootless. Detached. Disconnected. His cry to the Lord for deliverance expressed that ache within his soul:

Give Your attention to my cry,
For I have been brought very low;
Rescue me from my persecutors,
For they are too strong for me.
Bring my soul out of prison,
So that I may give thanks to Your name;
The righteous will surround me,
For You will look after me. (vv. 6–7)

His enemies were overwhelming to David. That cave felt like a prison to him—and he longed to be set free. He desperately desired a true home. A place where he could stop running. That prayer was eventually answered and David rose to the position of king for which he had been anointed so many years before, though at great cost—the death of his dearest friend, Jonathan the son of King Saul. As we will see, for seven and a half years David ruled in Hebron, but eventually the nation came together under his rule, as those loyal to the late King Saul withstood David's leadership for a time before finally coming on board to accept David's rule (2 Samuel 5:1–5).

Still, the former vagabond and current king needed a home from which to rule the entire nation. Years of wandering were answered by the call of that home. A home on a mountain. Mount Zion—which would become known as the city of David.

A Home for the King

An organization for which I have the highest regard is Habitat for Humanity. This nonprofit builds homes for people who have faced economic challenges, allowing those folks and their families to experience a key element of the American dream—homeownership. I've watched videos of people receiving the key to their first home (for which, by the way, they had to participate in the work of building it), and seeing the emotions involved in being a first-time homeowner is stunning.

For different reasons, I understand. The first fifteen years that Marlene and I were married, we pastored small churches for limited salaries. As a result, we rented. But, when we finally bought our first home, there was, I hope, an appropriate and understandable sense of pride. We were home. And we still have a picture of our little family—with the kids in some fairly crazy poses—standing by the Sold sign in the front yard. The smiles and excitement on our faces expose deep emotions that were very, very real.

What is it about home that affects us so viscerally? In a sense, it is all the things that David lacked when he was forced to flee from Saul as a fugitive. Stability. Roots. A sense of place. A sense of belonging. But there was more to it for David. The role of king was as demanding then as it is now, and he needed a solid base of operations.

The king was one of three Old Testament offices in Israel—and each had a specific role.

The prophet was God's representative to the people.

The priest was the people's representative to God.

The king was God's agent in leading the people. Remember, as we saw in chapter three, Israel was called to be a theocracy—a monarchy where God himself was the king. As such, the human king was God's agent in carrying out three important tasks:

1. Administering the welfare and affairs of the nation

2. Arbitrating disagreements among individuals (see Solomon and the two prostitutes in 1 Kings 3) to ensure the application of justice in the land

3. Assuring Israel's national security by leading the armies of Israel in battle

These were the tasks that awaited David as the new king of a reunited kingdom. As such, he needed a home from which to lead and rule—and the home he found was on a mountain.

In ancient times, cities were located on the basis of three criteria: access to trade routes, availability of water, and defensive positioning. Being on a high elevation helped expose any threats that might approach, which was a key element to the security of the city. Jerusalem fulfilled all of these criteria, so King David led his armies to that Jebusite city to make it his home and national headquarters:

> Now the king and his men went to Jerusalem against the Jebusites, the inhabitants of the land; and they said to David, "You shall not come in here, but even those who are blind and those who limp will turn you away," thinking, "David cannot enter here." Nevertheless, David captured the stronghold of Zion, that is, the city of David. (2 Samuel 5:6–7)

David and his troops laid siege to Jerusalem and conquered it, apparently entering the city secretly through Jerusalem's water tunnel (v. 8). Upon the conquest of Jerusalem, David laid specific claim to Zion (one of the hills of Jerusalem) and made it his personal enclave—so that it became known as the city of David. And, since no Jewish tribe had ever taken Jerusalem, it was a perfect place for David to situate his capital over all the tribes of Israel. *The Bible Knowledge Commentary* explains:

> Since Jerusalem had remained in Jebusite control ever since the days of Joshua (Josh. 15:63) it was considered neutral, so David's residence there would demonstrate tribal impartiality. But the very fact that Jerusalem had remained Jebusite indicated its security and defensibility.

Now firmly established as Israel's national capital, Jerusalem—particularly Mount Zion—formed a home for David and for the nation itself. His years of wandering were behind him. David's earthly story had brought him to Mount Zion and would eventually end on that mountain, the city of David (1 Kings 2:10). At home at last.

Zion's own story, however, had much more still to come. Over generations, Jerusalem became known as Israel's city of kings—and the center of Israel's eschatological hopes.

A Promise for the Future

Mount Zion became the home of Israel's human kings, but much more importantly, it became a symbol of God's own rule and kingship over Israel—which, after all, was a theocracy, not a simple monarchy. The website *Britannica.com* introduces us to some of the important facts about Mount Zion:

The etymology and meaning of the name are obscure. It appears to be a pre-Israelite Canaanite name of the hill upon which Jerusalem was built; the name "mountain of Zion" is common. In biblical usage, however, "Mount Zion" often means the city rather than the hill itself. *Zion* appears in the Old Testament 152 times as a title of Jerusalem; over half of these occurrences appear in two books, the Book of Isaiah (46 times) and that of Psalms (38 times). It appears seven times in the New Testament and five times in quotations from the Old Testament.

It is in those Scripture references that we find the implications of Zion's significance. Forty-six times the book of Isaiah mentions Zion, with a further thirty-eight times in the Psalms. In many of those cases, the prophet or the psalmist is reaching forward to the long game of God's kingship, promising a greater hope and a greater future.

It is no surprise that Isaiah, who so often mentions Zion, has more to say about the Messiah and Israel's future messianic hope than any other Old Testament book. Like the promises God gave Israel in Egypt, His promises to Israel for their ultimate future were also linked to the land—and uniquely to the rule and reign of God himself over the people from Mount Zion. This is why Isaiah 24:23 promises:

> For the LORD of armies will reign on Mount Zion and
>   in Jerusalem,
> And His glory will be before His elders.

The New Testament makes a similar connection for followers of Christ. Our future hopes are also intertwined with Zion, which is why Hebrews 12:22 tells us:

But you have come to Mount Zion and to the city of the living God, the heavenly Jerusalem, and to myriads of angels.

Written to Jewish believers, the book of Hebrews still identified Zion as the location where their hopes would eventually be realized—and we look forward to that realization as well. All of this was anticipated in one of the most important events during the public ministry of Jesus.

In His so-called triumphal entry, Jesus himself came to Zion.

In the triumphal entry, Jesus officially presented himself as Israel's messianic king. Every aspect of the event reached back into Israel's prophetic Scriptures, causing the gospel writer Matthew to describe the scene by citing Zechariah 9:9:

> **In the triumphal entry, Jesus officially presented himself as Israel's messianic king.**

Say to the daughter of Zion,
"Behold your King is coming to you,
Humble, and mounted on a donkey,
Even on a colt, the foal of a donkey." (Matthew 21:5)

In the euphoria of Jesus's entrance to Jerusalem, the people initially accepted Him as their rightful king as they shouted words from another messianic psalm—Psalm 118:

Hosanna to the Son of David;
Blessed is the One who comes in the name of the Lord;
Hosanna in the highest! (Matthew 21:9)

Hosanna means "save us, we pray!"—a cry fitting for the welcome of a king. This royal cry from ancient times was once again heard ringing down from Zion. As David had once climbed Mount Zion to establish his rule as king to save Israel from their enemies, David's greater son had come to Zion as well—in the name of the Lord. God had once more kept His promise, only a greater king than David was here—and a greater son was here. God's Son.

In spite of the celebratory atmosphere of that entry to Jerusalem, Jesus was eventually rejected and crucified. Still, there was a regal moment during the first Palm Sunday, as the King of Kings came to the city of kings and presented himself as the foundation for a different kind of kingdom. Jesus, the Rock of ages, laid down His life as the very foundation of this new kingdom when He gave himself on the cross, prompting Simon Peter to write:

For this is contained in Scripture:

"Behold, I am laying in Zion a choice stone, a precious cornerstone,
and the one who believes in Him will not be put to shame." (1 Peter 2:6; see Isaiah 28:16)

As the home of David, Mount Zion became the city of the king—but ultimately it will one day become the city of the King again. As Isaiah 52:7 promises:

How delightful on the mountains
Are the feet of one who brings good news,
Who announces peace
And brings good news of happiness,
Who announces salvation,
And says to Zion, "Your God reigns!"

Former slaving ship captain John Newton is best known as the author of the beloved hymn "Amazing Grace." But Newton also lifted his pen and his voice to celebrate the wonders of Zion—the rule of God and the kingship of Christ—in another classic hymn:

Glorious things of thee are spoken,
Zion, city of our God!
He, whose Word cannot be broken,
Formed thee for His own abode;
On the Rock of Ages founded,
What can shake thy sure repose?
With salvation's walls surrounded,
Thou mayst smile at all thy foes.

6

MOUNT CARMEL

An Invitation to Return

I grew up going to church, but my church tradition was not gospel- or Bible-oriented. As such, I struggled to understand a lot of concepts in the Bible. Baptism by immersion? What's up with that? Personal relationship with Christ? I had no clue. Verse-by-verse teaching of the Scriptures? What was the point of that? For me, many of these things were, to say the least, mysterious and, to say the most, confusing.

One of the ideas that seemed out of reach to me was repentance. I remember seeing newspaper cartoons of some scraggly hobo-looking dude on a sidewalk wearing a sandwich board declaring, "Repent . . . the end is near." I did not have the foggiest idea what that meant, or why it mattered. But it sure seemed ominous.

When I came to faith I began to gain a biblical and theological grounding to the issue of repentance, but it was much later in my walk with the Lord before I saw repentance practiced in an intensely personal way.

In March of 1995, I went to Moscow to spend a couple of weeks teaching pastors to help prepare them for ministry. The first Sunday, we were taken to a church that clearly preached the gospel. At the conclusion of the message, a young man came forward to give his life to Christ. In the States, in churches that give altar calls, I was accustomed to seeing someone go forward, say a quiet word to the pastor, be paired with a counselor, and then move to a prayer room for an intimate season of prayer during which, hopefully, they would receive Christ as their Savior.

In Moscow, and in the Russian evangelical church in general, it was dramatically different. When the young man went forward that morning, he knelt at the podium. The pastor then grabbed a microphone and put it in front of the young man's face and gave one word of instruction: "Repent." After a moment of silence, Russian words began to flow as, my interpreter told me, the young man began to express the wrongs he had done and the people he had hurt and the sins he had committed. While not in the quiet comfort of a designated prayer room, it was deeply moving and intimate in a different way. All of us were witnesses of his decision to turn from those things of sin and turn to Christ.

And that is the essence of repentance. It is a change of mind that produces a change of life. It is going one way and then turning to go another way. It is moving away from God, then turning and returning to Him. All of these expressions help to flesh out the Greek term *metanoia*, the New Testament word for "repentance." *Merriam-Webster Dictionary* says *metanoia* "means after-thought or beyond-thought, with *meta* meaning 'after' or 'beyond' (as in the modern word 'metaphysics') and *nous* meaning 'mind' (as in the modern world 'paranoia'). It is commonly understood as 'a transformative change of heart; especially: a spiritual conversion.'"

Put more simply, it is coming home to the Creator. It is a *turning* to Jesus that creates a *returning* to God—and one that He deeply desires for us to experience. As Paul told the church at Rome:

> It is a *turning* to Jesus that creates a *returning* to God.

Or do you think lightly of the riches of His kindness and restraint and patience, not knowing that the kindness of God leads you to repentance? (Romans 2:4)

God desires and welcomes our repentance—in fact, out of His rich kindness He calls us to return. And His great love welcomes us when we do.

One of the great Old Testament portrayals of repentance occurred on one of the most famous mountains of the Bible. And God led the people to the mountain in question by using some extreme measures—His kindness displayed in a surprising exhibition of His power.

The Backstory

In the health-care realm, two words that are almost always troubling are *chronic* and *systemic*. A health concern that is *chronic* has either remained for a long period of time or keeps coming back, despite treatments. A good example of this is seen in Mark 5 where Jesus encountered a woman with a bloody hemorrhage. For twelve long years, she labored under this debilitating condition, and in spite of continually seeking the medical help available at the time, her problem persisted. The "issue of blood" (v. 25 KJV) just stayed and stayed.

By contrast, a systemic issue spreads and grows until it affects the entire body. An example of systemic disease that has tragically impacted millions of women in our day is metastatic breast cancer, where the cancer which began in one part of the body spreads to the point where it overtakes other organs or systems within that body.

I have loved ones on both sides of that equation—battling both chronic and systemic health problems. These conditions can create an atmosphere of desperation coupled with despair.

This same reality applies in the spiritual realm. A cursory reading of the Old Testament reveals that Israel, the chosen people of God, had a spiritual problem that was both chronic and systemic. From the golden calf at the foot of Mount Sinai forward, Israel displayed a chronic vulnerability to idolatry. Once in the promised land, they were surrounded by pagan cultures with many gods—all of which seemed to attract Israel's devotion. Repeatedly, the people, seduced by these false gods, abandoned their calling as a people of the one true God to build places of worship in the "high places" (hilltops and mountains) to idols.

In fact, after Israel and Judah split from their status as one united kingdom under David's son Solomon to a divided land made up of two nations, the history of Judah (the Southern Kingdom) was defined by its kings—and the Scriptures identify those kings as good or bad depending on their response to the high places. While the bad kings encouraged, participated in, or ignored the idolatry of the people, the occasional good kings of the south, in most cases, tore down those high places in order to call the people back to God.

Israel (the Northern Kingdom), however, had no good kings. Only a steady succession of leaders whose constant intent was to draw the people away from God.

Enter King Ahab.

Not only did Ahab promote the worship of the god Baal, he married Jezebel, the daughter of a pagan king, and she, as a de facto priestess of Baal, imported that religious system into Israel. As such, the nation's chronic flirtations with idolatry deepened into a systemic problem that affected every area of life in the Northern Kingdom.

Who was this god Baal? *The Bible Knowledge Commentary* says,

> Baal (meaning "lord") is a name used generally in the Old Testament for the male deity the native Canaanite tribes worshiped under various other titles. The Tyrians called him Baal Melqart, but their religion was only a cultic variation of the standard Baal worship common throughout Palestine.

The New Bible Dictionary adds:

> Baal is called the son of Dagon. The texts reveal him as a nature deity; myths describe him in conflict with death, infertility and flood waters, emerging victorious as "king" of the gods.

In light of these references to nature and infertility (as opposed to fertility), some scholars see Baal as the god of weather or rain—the absolutely critical key to maintaining fertile farmlands in the ancient world. And King Ahab had imported Baal as the solution to Israel's agricultural concerns.

In 1 Kings 16, we see the depth of Ahab's rebellion against the God of his fathers—even to the point of building a temple to Baal in Israel's capital city of Samaria. Israel's idolatry moved from being both chronic and systemic to being institutionalized as national policy. The worship of Baal became the state religion.

So, God in His kindness responded in order to lead them to repentance. First Kings 17 introduces Elijah, God's prophet and representative, as he announced a drought that would encompass the land for three and a half years.

Drought.

Caused by lack of rain.

Which meant that the God of Israel was going to do battle with Israel's latest idol on Baal's own turf. If Baal was supposed to be the nature god who could provide what was needed for fertile farmland, God would call the people back by reminding them of the true Source of the rain. As Psalm 147:8 describes to us, God is the One

who covers the heavens with clouds,
Who provides rain for the earth,
Who makes grass sprout on the mountains.

And Psalm 68:9 affirms,

You made plentiful rain fall, God;
You confirmed Your inheritance when it was parched.

This was Israel's national heritage—yet they abandoned it to pursue the god of the moment, who promised but could not perform. And was exposed for it.

You might ask, But how could forty-two months of drought be an act of kindness on God's part? Because its purpose was to draw the people back to Him. To invite them to return. It was, in a sense, an extraordinary act of a God who lovingly and persistently pursued His people in order to call them home.

This purpose found its realization on yet another biblical mountain—Mount Carmel—where we will see what is sometimes called the battle of the gods.

The Battleground

The first time I led a study group to Israel, we landed at Tel Aviv's Ben Gurion Airport long after dark. I met up with our Israeli guide, and our weary, jet-lagged little group was loaded onto a bus and taken to our hotel where we crashed for the night.

The next morning at breakfast, I met with the guide to map our activities for the day. Rose was a delightful Jewish woman whose infectious laugh made it clear that she was going to be a lot of fun to work with for the next ten days. Once we finished, we got up to go to our rooms and collect our bags for the bus ride ahead, and on a sudden thought I asked Rose, "By the way, where are we?"

She laughed and said, "You don't know? Why, we are on Mount Carmel!"

What an extraordinary experience, to spend my first-ever night in Israel on one of the most famous locations in the

Scriptures. And it is famous because there Jehovah and Baal battled it out for the souls of the nation Israel. For three and a half years, drought—and its resulting famine—had raged in the land. Now, the time had come for this critical, nation-shaping event. Elijah challenged Ahab to a showdown to determine the true God of Israel, and the king accepted:

> So Ahab sent orders among all the sons of Israel and brought the prophets together at Mount Carmel. (1 Kings 18:20)

Mount Carmel is a deceptive name, because it is actually the name of a mountain range. Running from the Mediterranean Sea to the Valley of Megiddo, this topographical feature rises to some seventeen hundred feet of elevation. It is one of the most prominent features of that part of the Bible lands—dominating the scenery over which it towers. On one part of that range is a monument to Elijah that marks the traditional site of the epic battle now before us. To say it is impressive is to undersell the word *impressive*. It was one of the highest of the high places—and once again God was invading Baal's turf to take back His chosen people.

Facing up to a troop of some 450 Baal priests, the solitary Elijah set forth the question of the hour:

> Elijah approached all the people and said, "How long are you going to struggle with the two choices? If the LORD is God, follow Him; but if Baal, follow him." But the people did not answer him so much as a word. (v. 21)

The events that took place on Carmel were not a mere religious ritual or simply an intellectual exercise. It was an invitation to repentance—a call to turn from Baal and return to the God that Israel had abandoned.

You are probably familiar with the drama that unfolded on the mountain that day. The two sides agreed that they would each prepare a sacrifice and cry out to their respective god/God, and the one who answered with fire for the sacrifice would be established as Israel's one true deity. The Baal prophets prepared their sacrifice and began crying out to Baal for fire, but no fire came. As the morning wore on, their attempts became more desperate until, finally, Elijah challenged them:

> But there was no voice and no one answered. And they limped about the altar which they had made. And at noon Elijah ridiculed them and said, "Call out with a loud voice, since he is a god; undoubtedly he is attending to business, or is on the way, or is on a journey. Perhaps he is asleep, and will awaken." So they cried with a loud voice, and cut themselves according to their custom with swords and lances until blood gushed out on them. When midday was past, they raved until the time of the offering of the evening sacrifice; but there was no voice, no one answered, and no one paid attention. (vv. 26–29)

Honestly, if the scene weren't so tragic, it would be comically hilarious. But it *was* tragic for those Baal priests, for it exposed the utter impotence of their god before all the people who had been duped into giving their allegiance to this false idol.

So, Elijah prepared his altar and his sacrifice. In fact, Elijah trumped them by repeatedly drenching his sacrifice with water!

And he said, "Fill four large jars with water and pour it on the burnt offering and on the wood." And he said, "Do it a second time," so they did it a second time. Then he said, "Do it a third time," and they did it a third time. The water flowed around the altar, and he also filled the trench with water. (vv. 34–35)

Did you ever stop to think about that? They had just experienced three and a half years of drought, so where did they get all that water? I was standing on Mount Carmel near the Elijah monument when the only reasonable solution occurred to me—with no water in the land, it had to be hauled up from the Mediterranean Sea! Those four water vessels had to be taken down the mountain and carried back up three times to make sure no one could accuse Elijah of any trickery with his sacrifice.

Elijah's brief, almost understated prayer completed this activity:

Answer me, LORD, answer me, so that this people may know that You, LORD, are God, and that You have turned their heart back again. (v. 37)

It is extremely important to grasp the nuance of that prayer. While the Baal prophets were crying out for Baal to send fire, Elijah made no such specific request. This moment was about calling the people back to God. It was about an invitation to repent and return. So, Elijah prayed for God to make himself known to them—leaving the means of that revelation up to the wisdom of God himself. And God made himself known . . . with the fire Elijah had not verbally requested:

Then the fire of the LORD fell and consumed the burnt offering and the wood, and the stones and the dust; and it licked up the water that was in the trench. (v. 38)

The people had forsaken Jehovah to follow Baal, but God—like a loving father—pinched them in and made them see their frailty and weakness. He made them see their dependance and reliance on Him. He forced them to understand that Baal was not sufficient for the needs of their lives, but the God of Abraham, Isaac, and Jacob was—and forevermore would be.

So the people responded:

When all the people saw this, they fell on their faces; and they said, "The LORD, He is God; the LORD, He is God!" (v. 39)

God had challenged and chastened His people—but all for the purpose of inviting them to repent and return to Him. And they did.

The Beautiful Welcome

Have you heard the expression "You can't go home again"? For any of us who perhaps have had some times of difficulty with our parents or families, we know that returning home can be hard.

- Think of Jacob going home in Genesis 32–33 and knowing he had to face his brother Esau, whom he had defrauded.

- Think of the prodigal son in Luke 15 and the rehearsed speech he planned to give to his father. A speech acknowledging his unworthiness—yet he was desperate to come home again.

Those were difficult returns. Jacob had cheated his brother and knew he deserved whatever anger Esau still bore for him. The prodigal had brought shame and dishonor to his father in a culture where shame and honor were unbelievably important values, and he knew he did not deserve to be welcomed home.

But.

How might those returns have been less difficult had they known their return would be welcomed? The similarities of those welcomes are stunning:

Then Esau ran to meet him and embraced him, and fell on his neck and kissed him, and they wept. (Genesis 33:4)

So he set out and came to his father. But when he was still a long way off, his father saw him and felt compassion for him, and ran and embraced him and kissed him. (Luke 15:20)

Esau went to meet his brother and welcomed him home with embraces and kisses. The father raced through the village and welcomed his son home with embraces and kisses.

Yes, God had lovingly and patiently disciplined the people of Israel in order to draw them back to himself. So in a very real sense, they—like Jacob and the prodigal—*could* come home again knowing that they would be welcomed. And they did.

This is the good news the Scriptures offer to us. The events of Mount Carmel form one of Scripture's greatest pictures of God's loving patience to His wayward people, despite how far and how long they had drifted from Him. It was that self-same patience Peter reflected on in 2 Peter 3:9:

> The events of Mount Carmel form one of Scripture's greatest pictures of God's lovingpatience to His wayward people.

The Lord is not slow about His promise, as some count slowness, but is patient toward you, not willing for any to perish, but for all to come to repentance.

There it is—the beautiful welcome to repent and return to the God who made us in His image. The God who made us for eternity. The God who sees our waywardness and rebellion and invites us to come home anyway.

For the person who thinks, But you don't know what I've done . . . God could never forgive me, I point you to Carmel and the loving patience of the Father who called Israel back home despite chronic, systemic, even institutional spiritual failure.

This is the same God who not only calls us to come home again but paid the price to make that return possible. The old hymn "Come Thou Fount of Every Blessing" says this welcome home is part of how a person comes to Christ in the first place:

Jesus sought me when a stranger
Wandering from the fold of God;
He, to rescue me from danger,
Bought me with his precious blood.

Anyone who comes to the Father comes solely because of His provision through the precious blood of the cross and the resurrection of Jesus. It is not through religious effort or self-powered attempts at holiness. It is totally and completely about God providing what we could never accomplish on our own. That is how much He desires us to come home to Him.

And this is also God's heart for His children when we drift. Someone might say, "Yes, I trusted Jesus, but I've denied Him and dishonored Him. I've defied Him and defiled Him. How could it ever be possible for me to return home?" "Come Thou Fount" answers that question in a later verse that reaches out to acknowledge our brokenness and our frailty, even as children of God:

Prone to wander, Lord, I feel it,
Prone to leave the God I love.
Here's my heart, oh take and seal it,
Seal it for Thy courts above.

For those who don't yet know the Savior and for those who have wandered and drifted from God, Mount Carmel is a reminder that you can go home again—and your loving, forgiving heavenly Father will welcome you. He invites you to return.

7

Life in the Kingdom

For me, the best living, breathing example of a lifelong learner will always be Herb Vander Lugt. Herb had been a pastor for many years when he joined the staff of Radio Bible Class (now Our Daily Bread Ministries). When I met Herb, he was in his sixties and was writing for *Our Daily Bread* while serving as the ministry's senior research editor. Think about that—a research editor spends all day long researching. Wrestling with difficult biblical texts. Testing theological ideas. Learning. In his sixties.

Fifteen years later, when I joined the staff at Our Daily Bread, Herb was in his eighties and was still stretching himself—challenging himself to grow and learn. In one of life's surprising twists and turns, I found myself leading the team of which Herb was a member. This meant that, for several years, I had the daunting task of giving Herb his annual review. Now, it is important to be clear about this—it wasn't daunting because Herb was difficult. Just the opposite. It was daunting because I had no idea how to give a review to one of the wisest, most well-read, insightful, and gracious men I had ever known. It became a rare privilege, as I would spend most of our hour together testing ideas with Herb and listening to his stories.

There is something to be said for someone who never stops learning. Some say that when you stop learning, you stop living. Learning is that important.

In the secular realm, new ideas, emerging technologies, scientific exploration—all of these are important. In the realm of biblical endeavors, theological studies and hermeneutical theories continue to be honored pursuits. This is as it should be. There are few traits a person can have that are more valuable for life skills than a teachable spirit. A willingness to listen. To learn. To grow.

This is why Jesus's Great Commission is not simply about evangelism. While evangelism is the most widely regarded element of that commission, it also contains a challenge to teach so that those who come to the Savior can learn of Him and His heart and His ways.

Before returning to His Father, Jesus told His followers:

Go, therefore, and make disciples of all the nations, baptizing them in the name of the Father and the Son and the Holy Spirit, teaching them to follow all that I commanded you; and behold, I am with you always, even to the end of the age. (Matthew 28:19–20)

"Teaching them to follow" was not merely a catchy phrase. It was a reflection of one of the main priorities of Jesus's own earthly ministry. In fact, more than twenty times in Matthew alone we see Jesus actively teaching or referred to as a teacher, or people responding to His teaching.

Unsurprisingly, the teaching with which Jesus launched His public ministry is absolutely foundational to wise living. It is the indisputable starting point for a life that reflects the heart and spirit of the King we are called to know and serve. And Jesus took to a mountain to provide that initial teaching, appropriately known as the Sermon on the Mount.

The Start of Something Big

When you think about it, New Year's Day isn't really that big a deal. For the vast majority of the different areas of our lives, in the movement from December 31 to January 1 nothing actually changes except the last number in the year of the date. In most cases, you still work where you work. You still owe what you owe. You're still in the relationships you were in before. The shift from the final day of one year to the start of the next year actually amounts to one tick of the clock. One second. It truly isn't that significant.

Until you think about what the turning of that calendar page represents.

It represents a fresh start. A new beginning. An opportunity to go again. Beginnings are exciting (and perhaps a little terrifying). The start of a new football season. The beginning of a new school year. A new job. A wedding day. The birth of a baby. All of these starting points are significant. In a sense, from that moment forward, nothing will ever be the same again. After all, there is a reason we refer to graduation as "commencement." Though it is the end of something significant (a season of learning), it is the start of something new.

In a much more sweeping way, that is exactly the case with the beginning of Jesus's earthly ministry. Nothing would ever be the same again. Matthew's record of that starting point comes in a wave of events in Matthew 3 and 4. Jesus presented himself to John the Baptist for baptism and received a stunning endorsement from His heavenly Father (3:13–17). This was followed by a season of temptation in the wilderness where Jesus was tested by Satan—the first of several devilish attempts to derail the Christ from His certain purpose and mission (4:1–11). It was following that time of testing that Jesus began His ministry:

> From that time Jesus began to preach and say, "Repent, for the kingdom of heaven is at hand." (v. 17)

"Jesus began" is such an understated phrase that it is easy to miss the overpowering significance of this moment. Here it begins. For the first time, Jesus made the general public aware that something new had come. The proclamation of the kingdom's arrival then continued with the calling of the first disciples and Jesus's first displays of the power of God's kingdom come to earth. Some scholars say that, because of the Jews' reverence for the name of God and their unwillingness to speak it, "kingdom of heaven" became code for "kingdom of God." Heaven, as God's realm, became representative of the Father and His power.

So then, if the kingdom of God/heaven had arrived, was there evidence of that coming? Was the power of God visible in this new thing Jesus was announcing? Matthew answered that question:

Jesus was going about in all of Galilee, teaching in their synagogues and proclaiming the gospel of the kingdom, and healing every disease and every sickness among the people.

And the news about Him spread throughout Syria; and they brought to Him all who were ill, those suffering with various diseases and severe pain, demon-possessed, people with epilepsy, and people who were paralyzed; and He healed them. Large crowds followed Him from Galilee and the Decapolis, and Jerusalem, and Judea, and from beyond the Jordan. (vv. 23–25)

The combination of the declaration of the kingdom's arrival and the evidence of God's power drew people to Jesus. "Large crowds" gathered in wonder to see and hear what Jesus would do or say next.

Imagine—I know, it is beyond hard to imagine—the emotions of the crowds the first time they saw Jesus give sight to a blind person. The first leper restored to fresh, undiseased skin. The first demon-possessed person rescued. The news of these awe-filled events must have exploded throughout the villages surrounding the Sea of Galilee, drawing these crowds to Jesus—some perhaps to see if the stories were true, others maybe seeking relief for their own points of need. But, whatever their reasons, they came. And came. And came.

Now, with the assembled masses before Him, Jesus delivered the Sermon on the Mount. A new thing had begun with the call to the kingdom and the power of the kingdom. Now, Jesus followed that beginning with a manifesto of life in the kingdom. A manifesto given in a sermon delivered on a mountain.

A Place to Ponder

Do you have a quiet place? A place where you can sit, meditate, and reflect? In the busyness of my first trip to the Bible lands, our activities seemed like a blurring whirlwind with one amazing scene after another. One compelling site after another. One profound experience after another. Like drinking from the proverbial fire hydrant, I spent most of the first few days just trying to keep up (and I was leading the group!). More than anything else, I wanted a quiet place to process all that we had been experiencing.

That opportunity came when we stopped at the Church of the Beatitudes. Surrounded by lovely gardens and on the crest of a hill overlooking the beautiful waters of the Sea of Galilee, the church marks the traditional site of the Sermon on the Mount. We had our customary teaching time, and then I released the group to roam the gardens and enjoy the lovely spring day. I found a secluded bench where I could think and pray. I'll always warmly remember that mount as a place of peace, calm, and reflection.

While we don't know the exact location of the mountain where Jesus taught this landmark message, it seems to have been in the Galilee area (Matthew 4:23), perhaps near Capernaum, which became the headquarters for Jesus's activities in the northern regions of Israel. It wasn't hard for me to imagine Jesus sitting on the side of that hill and presenting His teaching. Matthew's brief description of the scene seems to me to be barely enough to capture this important moment of this most significant of beginnings:

When Jesus saw the crowds, He went up on the mountain; and after He sat down, His disciples came to Him. And He opened His mouth and began to teach them. (5:1–2)

With this statement, Matthew begins to build his telling of Jesus's story. Like each of the gospel writers, Matthew had a particular audience in mind and a particular method for communicating the story of Jesus to that audience. It is clear that Matthew, the former tax collector, was writing to a Jewish audience—which may explain the main structural feature for his gospel. Think about this:

> Moses used the five books of the Torah (the Pentateuch: Genesis, Exodus, Leviticus, Numbers, and Deuteronomy) to tell the story of God's call to and rescue of Israel, His chosen people.

> The ancient Jewish rabbis divided the book of Psalms into five books (1–31, 42–72, 73–89, 90–106, 107–150) to tell the story of what it is like to experience life in a fallen, broken world.

With that pattern firmly established in Israel's national memory, many scholars believe that Matthew used five major blocks of Jesus's teaching (5–7, 10, 13, 18, 23–25) as the spine around which he wrapped the story of Jesus.

With the first of those teaching times—the Sermon on the Mount—Matthew begins building his case for the kingship of the Christ.

The Big Idea of the Kingdom

When a new president is elected in the United States, there is a period of two and a half months before Inauguration Day.

For many, those are days of anticipation (or dread, depending on your party affiliation)—and one of the most anticipated moments is the new president's inaugural address. It is a very different kind of speech than the campaign messages of the previous months.

Campaign messages are largely about promises and policy. The inaugural address is about vision casting.

New presidents know that this speech is their opportunity to declare what they want America to become. Upon winning reelection, Abraham Lincoln longed for a season of healing in the final weeks of the War between the States. Franklin D. Roosevelt sought to give hope to a nation burdened with the weight of the Great Depression. John Kennedy presented the vision of a new generation exploring a new frontier. In each and every case, that first address set the tone for everything the new administration wanted to accomplish in the following years.

> The Sermon on the Mount was Jesus's inaugural address. In it, the King cast His vision for a kingdom that would be radically different.

In a sense, the Sermon on the Mount was Jesus's inaugural address. In it, the King cast His vision for a kingdom that would be radically different from anything that had ever been known by human beings. Yet, the difference was not just a political reality—the difference was about the character of the King which would define the character of His kingdom and everyone in it. If the kingdom of heaven was at hand, what would it look like?

The word that might best capture the nature of that new kingdom is *redefinition*. Throughout this opening address, Jesus repeatedly redefined everything the people of Israel thought they knew about what it meant to live in relationship with God.

Redefining the heart. The Beatitudes (Matthew 5:3–11) show the extraordinary difference of kingdom living as, first and foremost, living in a way that displays a heart that pleases the King. From Jesus's opening words, it was clear that this would be a speech unlike any other:

Blessed are the poor in spirit, for theirs is the kingdom of heaven. (v. 3)

Blessed are the poor? In what universe? Well, not in any universe—but in *His* kingdom? Yes. In the kingdom to which He had already begun calling people.

The Beatitudes laid out before the people the characteristics of a blessed life, not because it is lived in perpetual plenty and well-being but because it is lived with the heart of the kingdom. Jesus spoke in terms of stark realism. So, He spoke of poverty, mourning, hunger and thirst, and persecution (vv. 3–4, 6, 10–11).

But, Jesus's point was that those things in and of themselves do not define the kingdom—for it also includes gentleness, mercy, purity, and peace because it is lived out in the spirit of the King (vv. 5, 7–9). Jesus's kingdom is one where, under the rule of the King, there is a quality of life that shines through in the midst of *all* life's circumstances—not just the happy, joy-filled ones. The heart of the kingdom reflects the heart of its King.

Redefining the intent of the law. By the time of Jesus's ministry, the law had become something it had never been intended to be. It had become regulated ritual that was wielded like a weapon in order to shape behavior without necessarily transforming the heart. Jesus tackled this problem head-on in His inaugural message with the culturally shocking "you have heard it said . . . but I say to you . . ." section of the sermon. In each and every case, Jesus drilled down beneath the surface actions to the heart behind them.

> The action of murder finds its roots in a vengeful, hate-filled heart (5:21–26).

> The sin of adultery is born out of unbridled desire that is allowed to roam free (5:27–30).

> The action of divorce is indicative of deeper problems (5:31–32), and Jesus later explained that its roots are found in "hardness of heart" (19:8).

> Actions of revenge can only be resolved by embracing a heart of kindness and generosity (5:38–42).

> The self-motivated kind of love that only loves those who love us (or can help us) is to be overwhelmed by a heart that learns to love even its enemies (5:43–48).

This teaching from Jesus represented a fundamental reorganization of the values of the heart. It is the very essence of redefinition.

Redefining what relationship with God looks like. Nowhere is relationship with God experienced more intimately than in prayer—so Jesus modeled a kind of prayer that was radically different from those of the religious leaders to which the people were accustomed. This difference was found in the heart of the person doing the praying as well as in the nature of the prayer itself.

To that end, Jesus unpacked the unfortunate example of how those leaders were performing their religious duties to be honored by people, rather than so that people might honor God (6:1–8). This self-focused approach to their religion had made them into hypocrites, for their heart motives (continuing the previous theme of reorganized values) were not truly driven by love for God.

In that context, the prayer of the kingdom citizen was transformative:

> Our Father, who is in heaven,
> Hallowed be Your name.
> Your kingdom come.
> Your will be done,
> On earth as it is in heaven.
> Give us this day our daily bread.
> And forgive us our debts, as we also have forgiven our
>   debtors.
> And do not lead us into temptation, but deliver us from
>   evil. (vv. 9–13)

Unlike in the prayers with which the people were familiar, God himself was the first concern. His name. His kingdom. His will. The needs the kingdom citizen brought before this Father were real, practical, and daily—but also represented concern for others (*our* daily bread, not *my* daily bread) while seeking to maintain proper, unbroken relationships within the community of His kingdom.

And, just as we share in relationship with our Father and share in His provision of our daily bread, we share in a desire that He keep us (as a community) pure in the darkness of this world.

Defined by this prayer, relationship with God was no longer to be seen as an extension of religious activities. Jesus was redefining this relationship too into an experience that resembled a child going to their loving Father and finding in Him all that they need.

Redefining what wise living looks like. Psalm 111:10 offered:

> The fear of the LORD is the beginning of wisdom;
> All those who follow His commandments have a good
>   understanding;
> His praise endures forever.

The fear—awe, reverence—of the Lord was always intended to be the starting point for wise living. Psalm 111 states that idea in relationship to the law of Israel. Throughout the Sermon on the Mount, however, Jesus filled out His message with true wisdom for life that was redefined by being connected to the King himself—not the law of Moses. This kingdom wisdom called His listeners to higher ground as He called them to wisdom regarding all kinds of practical, everyday things:

Having an impact on the world around them as salt and light (Matthew 5:13–16)

The meaning of true righteousness, not a righteousness defined by ritualistic religion (5:20)

Caring for the poor (6:1–4)

Seeking to please God and God alone (6:16–18)

Discovering a heart of true contentment (6:19–24)

Attitudes of the heart that can defeat worry and anxiety (6:25–34)

Attitudes toward others and their brokenness (7:1–6)

Praying with an understanding of God's true heart (7:7–12)

Characteristics of a kingdom life (7:15–23)

That is an extraordinary catalog of powerful ideas—particularly realizing, again, that this was Jesus's inaugural kingdom message. Perhaps Jesus's entire call to this new wisdom can be encapsulated in one of the central verses of the address:

But seek first His kingdom and His righteousness, and all these things will be provided to you. (6:33)

This profound priority establishes solid ground for living as citizens of His kingdom. So foundational is this wisdom that, at the conclusion of this, His very first major address, Jesus boldly declared:

Therefore, everyone who hears these words of Mine, and acts on them, will be like a wise man who built his house on the rock. And the rain fell and the floods came, and the winds blew and slammed against that house; and yet it did not fall, for it had been founded on the rock. And everyone who hears these words of Mine, and does not act on them, will be like a foolish man who built his house on the sand. And the rain fell and the floods came, and the winds blew and slammed against that house; and it fell—and its collapse was great. (7:24–27)

Jesus concluded His Sermon on the Mount by telling the people that wisdom and foolishness had their own redefinition—they would now be understood in relationship to the words of the Christ. The Messiah. The King.

This was the message of the kingdom. It was the King casting a vision for all that His kingdom would do and be. It was Christ's own expression of the transformational work He intended to accomplish in the world—beginning in the hearts of those who would come to trust Him.

The people who heard this inaugural message responded to their ultimate teachable moment in an entirely appropriate way:

When Jesus had finished these words, the crowds were amazed at His teaching; for He was teaching them as one who had authority, and not as their scribes. (vv. 28–29)

The people were amazed. What about us? What does that transformed kingdom look like for us? And how will we respond to Christ's message about it?

The Big Idea for Us

We began this chapter by discussing the value of being lifelong learners, and that seems an immensely appropriate reminder as we pause to reflect on the Sermon on the Mount. In Romans 14:17, Paul—trained Jewish scholar that he was—acknowledged a different kind of kingdom than the one that had been built on the Mosaic law he had spent his life studying and applying. This new kingdom?

The kingdom of God is not eating and drinking, but righteousness and peace and joy in the Holy Spirit.

> As kingdom citizens, we allow the Spirit of the King to enable us to live out the heartand values of the King.

In other words, as we have been saying all along, life in the kingdom reflects the heart of the King. The descriptors Paul used to describe that heart are telling, to say the least:

Righteousness: right standing or relationship with God (2 Corinthians 5:21)

Peace: both peace with God (Romans 5:1) and peace from God (Philippians 4:7), as well as peace with one another (Romans 12:18)

Joy in the Holy Spirit: one commentator has described biblical joy as "choosing to respond to life's situations with inner contentment and satisfaction," which is a part of the overall expression of the fruit of the Spirit (Galatians 5:22–23)

These are elements of kingdom life that are both granted (through salvation and the provision of the Spirit) and learned as we grow in Christ and are made to be more like our King. And that is the big idea for us: as kingdom citizens, we allow the Spirit of the King to enable us to live out the heart and values of the King.

These values are heart-transforming realities that we never stop learning. In the things of our King, we are to be life-long learners who are shaped and molded to accomplish the Christlikeness that is God's ultimate and eternal intent for us:

> For those whom He foreknew, He also predestined to become conformed to the image of His Son. (Romans 8:29)

To that end, may we be receptive to the teaching work of our Lord and the Spirit—who came to guide and teach us (John 14:26). Or, as Benjamin M. Ramsey wrote in a fervent prayer:

> Teach me Thy way, O Lord, teach me Thy way!
> Thy guiding grace afford, teach me Thy way!
> Help me to walk aright, more by faith, less by sight;
> Lead me with heav'nly light, teach me Thy way!
>
> When I am sad at heart, teach me Thy way!
> When earthly joys depart, teach me Thy way!
> In hours of loneliness, in times of dire distress,
> In failure or success, teach me Thy way!
>
> When doubts and fears arise, teach me Thy way!
> When storms o'erspread the skies, teach me Thy way!
> Shine through the cloud and rain, through sorrow, toil,
>   and pain;
> Make Thou my pathway plain, teach me Thy way!

Long as my life shall last, teach me Thy way!
Where'er my lot be cast, teach me Thy way!
Until the race is run, until the journey's done,
Until the crown is won, teach me Thy way!

8

MOUNT OF TRANSFIGURATION

Father and Son

One of the biblical texts that has fascinated me over the years is Ephesians 3:20–21, which reads:

> Now to him who is able to do immeasurably more than all we ask or imagine, according to his power that is at work within us, to him be glory in the church and in Christ Jesus throughout all generations, for ever and ever! Amen. (NIV)

I have repeatedly written, taught, and preached on this magnificent text—and why not? It is one of the most majestic doxologies in all of the New Testament. It has a depth of wonder about the greatness of our God that deserves to be explored over and over again. As the title of the popular praise chorus affirms, "How Great Is Our God." And Ephesians 3:20–21 was declaring that greatness long before there were any praise choruses.

For me, however, the part where I always get hung up is the phrase "more than all we ask or imagine." I have a pretty vivid imagination, and I can imagine a lot! But that claim is quickly checked because the Scriptures remind me of my shortsightedness. I find it hard to shake Paul's affirmation of wonder in Romans 11:33–36:

> Oh, the depth of the riches, both of the wisdom and knowledge of God! How unsearchable are His judgments and unfathomable His ways! For who has known the mind of the Lord, or who became His counselor? Or who has first given to Him, that it would be paid back to him? For from Him, and through Him, and to Him are all things. To Him be the glory forever. Amen.

Even the apostle Paul, with one of the greatest minds our God has ever invested into the church, struggled to grasp the magnitude and majesty of the Creator and His purposes. Yet, while plenty of biblical evidence abounds to remind me that the wisdom and power and glory of our God are beyond my imagination, where I really confront this unimaginable greatness face-to-face is when I join Peter, James, and John on the slow climb up the mountain where they witnessed the transfiguration of Jesus. Matthew's account of this titanic event begins with these simple words:

> Six days later, Jesus took with Him Peter and James, and his brother John, and led them up on a high mountain by themselves. (17:1)

In our journey through key biblical events that took place on mountaintops, we have seen some fairly spectacular moments in the Bible story. Think of where we have been together so far:

The slow cessation of the great flood

The sudden provision of a lamb

The determined giving of the law

The tragic consequences of foolish choices

The establishment of a home for the king (and the King)

The battle of the God of Israel versus Baal

The presentation of the manifesto of the kingdom of God

Each of these events is extraordinary in its own right. But, at least for me, none of those scenes rise to the level of being unimaginable. In my mind's eye I can craft a portrayal of those events because, quite frankly, they include such decisively human elements.

When we ascend the Mount of Transfiguration, however, we touch the eternal. We witness the divine. We glimpse a sight with no earthly frame of reference, because in the transfiguration, we see heaven revealed on earth. It is shocking and awe-inspiring and terrifying. Even in the modern world of computer-generated graphics where the unthinkable is regularly visualized, there is no meaningful parallel to the moment where the glory of the Son of God was revealed to His three overwhelmed disciples.

And so, for the purpose of full disclosure, I must confess my utter inadequacy to tackle the scene that is before us.

But tackle it we must. It is too important to ignore and too meaningful to fail to wrestle with. The final book of the Bible is formally titled "The Revelation of Jesus Christ" (Revelation 1:1). But the first revelation—which means "to unveil or make visible"—of Jesus Christ in His matchless, breathtaking glory took place on a mountain. This truly qualifies as the proverbial, prototypical mountaintop experience.

So, I almost feel that, like Moses, I should take the shoes off my feet for we are stepping together onto holy ground. The Mount of Transfiguration.

How Did We Get Here?

Once again, context is everything. Words that might seem unkind in one context make perfect sense and even become compassionate in a different setting. As we've seen, in biblical studies context is even more important. Any event or statement must be framed by what surrounds it if we are to even begin to grasp its meaning.

We find the context of Christ's transfiguration in Matthew 16, which seems to be about in the middle of Jesus's three or so years of public ministry. In that chapter, two significant events happen, and both deserve our careful attention.

The first of these events took place when Jesus walked His disciples from Galilee to Caesarea Philippi. The most northern point of Israel, Caesarea Philippi stood at the base of Mount Hermon and, because of its remoteness, had been developed as a retreat for Roman soldiers to escape the heat and pressures of Jerusalem for a small taste of home. Roman temples, businesses, food, and comforts were readily available, and Caesarea Philippi became a thoroughly Roman outpost in a region the legions were finding so difficult to police and control.

There, Jesus took His disciples and, against the backdrop of the gods of the world, asked them two questions:

Who do people say that the Son of Man is? (v. 13)

And . . .

But who do you yourselves say that I am? (v. 15)

The first question, in that context, was intended to elicit the Jewish viewpoint regarding the question of Jesus's identity in a place surrounded by the gods of the world. The second question was to confirm that His followers understood the miracles and authoritative teachings they had seen and heard while following Jesus. Peter provided the response to the second of those questions:

You are the Christ, the Son of the living God. (v. 16)

This affirmation closed the first half of Jesus's public ministry, which proved to His disciples *who* He was. Peter's words made it clear that Jesus's identity had been revealed, so it was time for Him to begin the second half of His ministry. The first half of our Lord's ministry was occasionally private with the Twelve, but it mostly focused on the crowds that flocked to Him. This second half would be more intimate, focused on preparing the Twelve for what was coming in Jesus's passion.

For that reason, immediately following Peter's declaration, Jesus—for the very first time—explained to His followers *why* He had come. He revealed that His eventual trip to

Jerusalem would lead to the suffering and sacrifice that must take place there. And not just any suffering or sacrifice: His own suffering and sacrifice.

> From that time Jesus began to point out to His disciples that it was necessary for Him to go to Jerusalem and to suffer many things from the elders, chief priests, and scribes, and to be killed, and be raised up on the third day. (v. 21)

Although this was the very first time Jesus unfolded His true mission for these followers, He would explain it further two more times (17:22–23; 20:17–19) as He sought to prepare them for what was on the horizon. Then, following a challenge from Peter (16:22–23) and a description of the true nature of discipleship (vv. 24–27), Matthew 16 closes with these words of Jesus:

> Truly I tell you, there are some of those who are standing here who will not taste death until they see the Son of Man coming in His kingdom. (v. 28)

This is the statement that precedes the events of the transfiguration. This is what Matthew wanted to have ringing in our ears as we approach chapter 17, for many see the Mount of Transfiguration as the immediate fulfillment of that remarkable promise.

What Do We See Here?

There is a real danger that we can look at things, moments, people, or events and yet not really *see* them. Whether the problem is not seeing the proverbial forest for the trees or missing the grandeur of a single tree because we are trying to absorb the vastness of the forest, we are constantly in danger of viewing life in such a way that we miss the value and benefit that any particular moment affords.

I learned that lesson from a pastor who ministered to me in my early days as a follower of Jesus. He had a profound global ministry that often saw him speaking to thousands of people at a time, but he also had a great heart and great compassion for people as individuals. As a result, in spite of the throngs that came to hear him, he never lost sight of those who made up the audiences. When he looked out onto a crowd, he didn't just see people—he saw *persons*.

When we approach the transfiguration of Jesus, we cannot afford to fail in our seeing. To be fair, there are lots of things to capture our attention. The three inner-circle disciples (Peter, James, and John) were there and, as was often the case, Peter did something that would distract our attention. Additionally, Elijah and Moses were present there. These two heroes of Israel, as we have seen, had their own mountaintop experiences, yet here they were at the transfiguration of Jesus. Elijah, who called the people back to their God, and Moses, who was prohibited from entering the promised land until this very moment (see chapter 3), would easily capture our attention if we let them.

But, while not ignoring these important components to the story, it is critical that we do not miss what matters most. What the three fishermen saw. What we need to see: the glory of the King of Kings on display.

Matthew, in a master class of understatement, described the scene as we join them on the mountain. And while the actual mountain where the transfiguration occurred remains a mystery (Mount Tabor is the traditional site), the event itself was the revealing of the utmost mystery: having declared Jesus's *identity* at Caesarea Philippi, Peter and his friends were now confronted by Jesus's true *nature*!

> Six days later, Jesus took with Him Peter and James, and his brother John, and led them up on a high mountain by themselves. And he was transfigured before them; and His face shone like the sun, and His garments became as white as light. And behold, Moses and Elijah appeared to them, talking with Him. (17:1–3)

It is the word *transfigured* that takes this entire happening to a next level of understanding for us. The Greek word here is *metamorphosis*, which describes a dramatic and drastic change in form. The apostle Paul used this term to describe how our lives are transformed into the likeness of Christ in Romans 12:2 and 2 Corinthians 3:18, yet there seems to be an enormous, indescribable qualitative difference between the transformation we undergo as Christ followers and the one Jesus displayed on the mountain.

When we are transformed, it is from what we *were* to what we are *becoming* in Christ. As Paul put it, "But we all, with unveiled face, looking as in a mirror at the glory of the Lord, are being transformed into the same image from glory to glory, just as from the Lord, the Spirit" (2 Corinthians 3:18).

Now, don't get me wrong—that is magnificent. God, by His Spirit, is working to transform us to become more and more like Jesus. It is a priceless privilege and an amazing gift that God gives us as the result of our salvation.

But, for Jesus, transfiguration was eternally so much more. Jesus was not transformed from what He *was* to what He was *going to become*. Not at all. When Jesus was transfigured, He was transformed from what He had *temporarily become*—a true human being—to what He had *always been* from eternity past—the second person of the Godhead. This is the true revelation of Jesus before His disciples, who must have been thoroughly shattered by what they were witnessing.

As Pastor Warren Wiersbe wrote:

> As far as the record is concerned, this is the only time Jesus revealed His glory in this way while He was on the earth. . . . Our Lord's glory was not *reflected* but *radiated* from within. There was a change on the outside that came from within as He allowed His essential glory to shine forth (Hebrews 1:3).
>
> Certainly this event would strengthen the faith of the disciples, particularly Peter, who had so recently confessed Jesus to be the Son of God. Had Peter made his confession *after* the Transfiguration, it would not have been so meaningful. Peter believed, confessed his faith, and then received assurance (see John 11:40; Hebrews 11:6).

The transfiguration served as an exclamation point to Peter's declaration in Matthew 16. The Christ, the Son of the living God, was suddenly unveiled to the disciples as affirmation of the truth of that title. This event so powerfully affected them that both Peter and John continued to ponder this matchless moment years after it occurred:

And the Word became flesh, and dwelt among us; and we saw His glory, glory as of the only Son from the Father, full of grace and truth. (John 1:14)

> **The Christ, the Son of the living God, was suddenly unveiled to the disciples.**

When did they see that glory? On the Mount of Transfiguration. Peter reflected on the same event in his second letter:

For we did not follow cleverly devised tales when we made known to you the power and coming of our Lord Jesus Christ, but we were eyewitnesses of His majesty. For when He received honor and glory from God the Father, such a declaration as this was made to Him by the Majestic Glory: "This is My beloved Son with whom I am well pleased"—and we ourselves heard this declaration made from heaven when we were with Him on the holy mountain. (1:16–18)

"Eyewitnesses of His majesty." That is a truly mind-boggling statement. Remember, these disciples had been with Jesus. They had seen Jesus walking, eating, sleeping, and living. They had seen Him weary, hungry, thirsty, and determined. They had witnessed Him teaching, healing, rescuing, and comforting.

But they had never seen *this*.

They had never seen what Peter later called "Majestic Glory," What was this?

The Hebrew word for "glory" in the Bible literally means weightiness, substance, and significance. The glory of God, as such, speaks of His utter significance that surpasses anything else in the universe in importance. Some scholars see God's glory as the expression of the sum total of the perfections of His attributes, and the Scriptures normally depict that glory as a bright, brilliant light. But when Moses asked to see God's glory, God showed him only His goodness—and it was overwhelming to the Israelite leader (Exodus 33:18–19). Here, the full force of the glory of the Christ was put on display for Peter, James, and John.

In a word, this revealed glory is an unveiling of God as the primary One. What older theologians called "the divine Other." The One who is so decidedly different from us that, when we see Him as He is, we should fall at His feet. Certainly, that is what John did in Revelation 1:17 when, on the isle of Patmos, he found himself in the presence of the risen, glorified Jesus. This divine otherness is what makes God *transcendent*—literally, too far beyond us for us to reach.

Why does that matter? It matters because this God—who is transcendent and beyond us—nevertheless chose to come near, not simply by coming among us but by actually *becoming* one of us. Just thinking that this God would become like us because of His great love for us is beyond imagination. No wonder John found himself simply saying, "God is love" (1 John 4:8).

This revelation of Jesus's glory is worth sitting with and reveling in.

But perhaps the least surprising element of the story occurs when Peter, not knowing what to say (Mark 9:6), spoke up anyway:

> Lord, it is good that we are here. If You want, I will make three tabernacles here: one for You, one for Moses, and one for Elijah. (Matthew 17:4)

I love Peter and his compulsive, knee-jerk approach to life. He feels very familiar to me. But remember, Jesus had to lovingly correct Peter in Matthew 16:23 when Peter reacted strongly to Jesus's prediction of His coming death and resurrection. Now, a truly remarkable thing happened as God the Father himself moved in to correct Peter!

> While he was still speaking, a bright cloud overshadowed them, and behold, a voice from the cloud said, "This is My beloved Son, with whom I am well pleased; listen to Him!" (17:5)

There it is—the corrective my heart needs regularly. The reminder that the Author and Finisher of my faith is where my attention needs to be focused is a reminder for the ages (Hebrews 12:2 NKJV). Especially for those of us so easily distracted by the shiny bells and piping whistles the surrounding culture continually throws in front of us.

Look to Jesus.

Listen to Jesus.

Allow the glorious, preeminent Jesus to be preeminent in each of us.

It appears that Peter and his companions got the message, for Matthew continues:

> When the disciples heard this, they fell face down to the ground and were terrified. And Jesus came to them and touched them and said, "Get up, and do not be

afraid." And raising their eyes, they saw no one except Jesus Himself alone. (17:6–8)

As always, when the disciples were troubled or disturbed or, as here, rightly terrified, Jesus spoke peace to them. In His now-familiar presence, they found themselves covered with His now-familiar peace. And they continued the movement that was ultimately resolved in the cross of Christ.

As we have seen, Jesus was beginning the second half of His ministry, and the transfiguration was the Father's own sign-off on that mission. In calling Jesus His "beloved Son," the Father essentially gave the same affirmation that He had given at the launch of the first half of Jesus's ministry. At His baptism, Matthew recorded these words:

> And a voice from the heavens said, "This is My beloved Son, with whom I am well pleased." (3:17)

Both halves of Jesus's ministry received the Father's approval and endorsement—as the Father and the Son together worked for the rescue of lost humanity. Now, Jesus moved ever closer to the cross, and the fulfillment of His mission.

But Peter, James, and John were left with a staggering memory that would never be far from their hearts—marking them indelibly even as they grew old and wrote of their experiences with the Christ.

What Does It All Mean?

One of the most pervasive aspects of Christian thinking in our day is that everything in the Bible has to somehow apply to me. To my life. To my situation. Yet, like Peter, we would do well to remember that Jesus himself is the main character of this drama—and we are to focus on and listen to Him.

So, rather than asking what this event means *to me*, maybe the more important question is, What does it mean? What does it tell us about Jesus? About His Father?

Yes, it makes a profound statement that this transcendent Christ loved us so much that He came to us.

Yes, it is vitally important that this Christ—the One who is himself Majestic Glory—was willingly shamed, humiliated, and disgraced as He bore our sins in His body on the cross (1 Peter 2:24).

> Christ—the One who is himself Majestic Glory— was willingly shamed, humiliated, and disgraced as He bore our sins in His body on the cross.

And yes, it is wonderful to consider that the One who was transfigured on that dark mountain made it possible for us to be transformed by the renewing of our minds (Romans 12:2).

I am eternally grateful for those benefits that we have in Christ. But, for this moment, I think it is enough to focus on Him. On His greatness. On His glory. On His majesty. On His perfection. On His mercy. On His love. On His power. On His kindness.

On Him.

To simply bow in worship and give honor to the One who was and is and is forevermore. As hymn writer Robert Grant so powerfully put it in his hymn of the divine Other:

O worship the King, all glorious above,
And gratefully sing His power and His love;
Our Shield and Defender, the Ancient of Days,
Pavilioned in splendor, and girded with praise.

O tell of His might, O sing of His grace,
Whose robe is the light, Whose canopy space,
Whose chariots of wrath the deep thunderclouds form,
And dark is His path on the wings of the storm.

Frail children of dust, and feeble as frail,
In Thee do we trust, nor find Thee to fail;
Thy mercies how tender, how firm to the end,
Our Maker, Defender, Redeemer, and Friend.

9

"MOUNT" CALVARY

Love on Display

Some of the most beloved hymns of the Christian faith have to do, obviously, with the events surrounding the cross and what Jesus accomplished there. And, running through those beloved lyrics, we discover a rather consistent subtheme:

> Up Calv'ry's mountain, one dreadful morn,
> Walked Christ my Savior, weary and worn.
> ("Blessed Redeemer," Avis B. Christiansen)

> One day they led Him up Calvary's mountain,
> One day they nailed Him to die on the tree.
> ("One Day," J. Wilbur Chapman)

> On a hill far away stood an old rugged cross,
> The emblem of suff'ring and shame.
> ("The Old Rugged Cross," George Bennard)

I have clear and happy memories of listening as a boy to my dad's favorite album of hymns and trying to understand the depth of my own emotions that were stirred by hearing Tennessee Ernie Ford's rich baritone voice sing "The Old Rugged Cross"—a hymn that affects me greatly still to this day.

In somewhat more recent years, there are other similar songs like "I Believe in a Hill Called Mount Calvary," written by Bill and Gloria Gaither and Dale Oldham, and "The Day He Wore My Crown" by Phil Johnson.

Over and over, Christian music both past and present describes the site of the heartbreaking happenings of the crucifixion and death of the Lord Jesus Christ as a hill or a mountain or a mount. For our purposes, that all seems very appropriate, since we have been looking together at mountains in the Bible and the momentous things connected with those dark hours. Certainly the events of the cross qualify as momentous.

But one thing all those loved and accepted songs have in common is that they share an assumption that isn't clearly supported by the Scriptures.

Nowhere in the Bible are we told that Calvary was on a hill or a mountain.

If you were paying close attention, you may have noticed that the title to this chapter is "'Mount' Calvary." You may have even wondered why the word *Mount* was in quotation marks. Now you know.

Although several consistently reliable New Testament commentaries insist on calling Golgotha a hill, the four gospels simply refer to it as a "place" called "the Skull." The translation "skull" comes from the Greek word *kraniou*, which is the equivalent of the Aramaic word *golgotha* or the Latin word *calvary*. That terminology is consistent in the Gospels, though any thought of the crucifixion site being an elevated space is missing from the text:

- Matthew 27:33: "And when they came to a place called Golgotha, which means Place of a Skull . . ."

- Mark 15:22: "Then they brought Him to the place Golgotha, which is translated, Place of a Skull."

- Luke 23:33: "When they came to the place called The Skull, there they crucified Him and the criminals, one on the right and the other on the left."

- John 19:17: "They took Jesus, therefore, and He went out, carrying His own cross, to the place called the Place of a Skull, which in Hebrew is called, Golgotha."

The Christian tradition of referring to Calvary as a hill or mount apparently started during the sixth century after the birth of Christ. The Scriptures simply tell us that it was called "Place of a Skull" and that it was "outside the gate" of the city of Jerusalem (Hebrews 13:12).

So, then, what are we to make of this interesting challenge?

Why This Tradition?

When I have led study groups to Israel, we spend one of our days in Jerusalem with a focus on Jesus's passion. We begin at the base of the Mount of Olives in the garden of Gethsemane. Among the ancient, gnarled olive trees, we have a brief devotional time of prayer before roaming the gardens for a few moments, contemplating the agony our Savior endured there. Following a series of other sites (like the Via Dolorosa—the traditional path Jesus walked on His way to the place of crucifixion), we arrive at the Garden Tomb area.

Why that particular location rather than the Church of the Holy Sepulchre, another traditionally held site for the suffering and burial of Jesus? Several reasons give weight to the Garden Tomb site. First, as we saw earlier, Hebrews 13:12 says that Jesus was crucified "outside the gate"—that is, outside the perimeter walls of Jerusalem proper—and the Garden Tomb fits the bill.

Additionally, John 19:41–42 tells us,

Now in the place where He was crucified there was a garden, and in the garden was a new tomb in which no one had yet been laid. Therefore because of the Jewish day of preparation, since the tomb was nearby, they laid Jesus there.

The Garden Tomb area is, in fact, a garden with an ancient tomb carved from the limestone walls that surround it. Additionally, the place of Jesus's crucifixion was a place of constant travel because those "passing by" were pausing long enough to hurl mockery and abuse at Him (Matthew 27:39). Ironically, the Garden Tomb site is today located next to a major bus terminal that services Jerusalem and fronts a major road into the city used since ancient times.

But, the dominant reason for viewing the Garden Tomb area as a strong possibility for the location of these events is that word *skull* to which we have been giving so much attention. Directly beside the Garden Tomb enclave is a rough hill where you can easily imagine the vacant eye sockets, nose, and forehead of a skull in the face of that small knob of a hill. First suggested as a potential site for the cross by a German scholar in the 1840s, that high place became better known as Gordon's Calvary after British Major-General Charles Gordon noted the skull-like appearance of the hill in the 1880s. This identification of the location followed the discovery of the Garden Tomb itself in the 1860s—which seemed to fulfill the few scant details the Scriptures do provide for us.

Still, even the usage of the word *skull* is marked by some mystery. The *Tyndale Bible Dictionary* offers this:

> The reason why this place was called "the skull" is unknown, although several explanations have been offered. An early tradition, apparently originating with Jerome (AD 346–420), asserted that it was a common place of execution and that the skulls of many who had been executed were strewn around the site. No first-century evidence has been found to substantiate this viewpoint. Some suggest that it was a place of execution and that "skull" was used figuratively, simply as a symbol of death. Origen (AD 185–253) mentioned an early, pre-Christian tradition that the skull of Adam was buried in that place. This is probably the oldest explanation of the name, and is referred to by several writers after Origen. Others have said that the name resulted from the fact that the place of the Crucifixion was a hill that had the natural shape of a skull. No early evidence from any sources has been found to substantiate this view, and the NT accounts do not refer to the place as a hill.

Like several of the mountains we have looked at together, we simply do not have certainty about the precise location where the events of the cross took place.

So, then, where does that leave us?

Why Does This Matter?

There is an old expression that "the devil is in the details." I prefer a more worthy spin on that phrase that affirms that "God is in the details." In that sense, there is no unimportant detail in the Scriptures. There is no slapdash, indifferent moment. No inconsequential truth or event. And that includes the details of what the Scriptures do—and do not—tell us about. And that includes the detail of whether Golgotha was or was not a mountain.

Although there is no biblical evidence to that end, Christian tradition has long held that Golgotha was a hill of some kind. Why has there been so much allegiance to such an uncertain idea?

First of all, Jerusalem itself is built on a collection of mountaintops—explaining why, like Rome, it is sometimes referred to as a "city on seven hills." This location makes Jerusalem the highest point in the south of Israel, rising some 2,474 feet above sea level. In part, the lofty elevation of the city is why the Bible always speaks of "going up" to Jerusalem—it is both a physical reality and a spiritual metaphor for going up to worship in the presence of God.

The rise of the mountains of Jerusalem above the Jericho plain is the reason for the subset of psalms known as the Songs of Ascent (Psalms 120–134). These particular songs were collected so that people could sing them as they made their annual pilgrimages *up* to Jerusalem for the three primary feasts of Israel (Passover, Firstfruits, and Tabernacles). Still today, when Jewish pilgrims travel from around the world to their ancient homeland, they refer to it as *aliyah* or "going up."

That is all well and good. There may or may not have been a skull-shaped hill, and this "going up" may or may not be a reference to the general mountainous area in which Jerusalem rests. We don't know.

What we do know, however, is that, whether the actual physical location was a hill or not, the events that occurred on Calvary are undeniably the true, real summit of God's rescuing work. Jesus's crucifixion at the place of the skull, where He paid for sin and restored the way home to the Father, is described with almost painful minimalism in Mark's gospel:

> Then they brought Him to the place Golgotha, which is translated, Place of a Skull. And they tried to give Him wine mixed with myrrh; but He did not take it. And they crucified Him. (15:22–24)

They crucified Him.
Jesus.
The Son of God.
On a cross.

By willingly submitting himself to the most agonizing death ever imagined by the wicked hearts of sinful human beings, the Lamb of God took away the sins of the world. Jesus's suffering was so indescribable that His method of execution even generated a word intended to reflect unmeasured anguish—*excruciating*. The middle of that word ("cruci") derives from the word *crucifixion*, making the cross forever stand as the absolute standard for unimaginable suffering.

On the cross, God entered into suffering with us and forever redeemed it. Peter Kreeft rightly said, "Jesus is the tears of God." Henri Nouwen concluded that "God wanted to liberate us, not by removing suffering from us, but by sharing it with us." Jesus is "God-who-suffers-with-us," most clearly seen in the cross. Perhaps that is why George MacLeod wrote:

> Jesus was not crucified in a cathedral between two candles, but on a cross between two thieves; on the town garbage heap; at a crossroad so cosmopolitan they had to write his title in Hebrew and in Greek and in Latin; at the kind of place where cynics talk smut and soldiers gamble. Because that is where he died. And that is what he died about.

The reality of the suffering Savior as God-who-suffers-with-us prompted John Stott to say, "I could never myself believe in God, if it were not for the cross. The only God I believe in is the One Nietzsche ridiculed as 'God on the cross.' In the real world of pain, how could one worship a God who was immune to it?"

> On the cross, God entered into suffering with us and forever redeemed it.

Amy Carmichael adds, "There are times when nothing holds the heart but a long, long look at Calvary. How very small anything that we are allowed to endure seems beside that Cross."

God loves us with an everlasting love. Followers of Christ can embrace this with hope and confidence, and offer it to a world suffering more than we can imagine. We do not offer creeds or ideologies, theories or theologies. In the end, we offer Jesus, God-who-suffers-with-us.

That is why Jesus's agony on the cross was, at the risk of sounding trivial, the Mount Everest of God's work in the world. The horrific cross of torture and humiliation became what Isaac Watts described as the "wondrous cross on which the Prince of Glory died." The darkness and despair of crucifixion day was transformed into "Good" Friday—not because of what was done to Jesus there, but rather because of what He accomplished. The tragedy of the crucified Christ became the glory of all who would be redeemed through His sacrifice.

As a result, Paul, rather than simply mourning the cross (an act that is not altogether inappropriate in its own right), realized and even celebrated the immense worth of the cross. The eternal value of the cross. The unmitigated glory of the cross. His reflections on the cross tell their own story of wonder, awe, and worship:

> For the word of the cross is foolishness to those who are perishing, but to us who are being saved it is the power of God. (1 Corinthians 1:18)

> But far be it from me to boast, except in the cross of our Lord Jesus Christ, through which the world has been crucified to me, and I to the world. (Galatians 6:14)

> . . . and through Him to reconcile all things to Himself, whether things on earth or things in heaven, having made peace through the blood of His cross. (Colossians 1:20)

Peter, the disciple of denial, also reflected on the cross when he wrote, "And He Himself brought our sins in His body up on the cross, so that we might die to sin and live for righteousness; by His wounds you were healed" (1 Peter 2:24).

There is not now nor could there ever be any higher ground than the display of love God put forth at Skull Place in Jerusalem on that climactic day two thousand years ago, a truth affirmed by Romans 5:8: "But God demonstrates His own love toward us, in that while we were still sinners, Christ died for us."

The cross is the apex.

The zenith.

The peak above all other mountains.

Whether Calvary was on a hill or not.

How Does It All Fit?

Before time began, the eternally wise God knew that creation would bring failure, brokenness, and sin. He knew a sacrifice would be required to put things right again. And He knew His Son would be the Lamb for that ultimate sacrifice. I love the way John's description of Jesus reads in the King James Version:

> . . . the Lamb slain from the foundation of the world. (Revelation 13:8)

This was the plan all along. The Bible was given to tell us this eternal story. The story of God's rescuing love began in the backwash of our first parents' failure in Eden when God promised them that a Victor would come (Genesis 3:15). This promise was behind all that followed in the Old Testament.

It is the greatest story ever told.

The story of Jesus.

As Sally Lloyd-Jones says of the stories of the Bible, "Every story whispers His name."

I believe that with all my heart.

The "Place of a Skull" is the necessary and worthy climax for the story that the Bible tells. Everything in the Bible either looks forward to the cross of Calvary with anticipation or looks back on it with reflection—and that includes the stories told on the mountains we have been considering together:

> Everything in the Bible either looks forward to the cross of Calvary with anticipation or looks back on it with reflection.

Like Ararat, Calvary offers a second chance to a broken, rebellious humanity—but this second chance is both for now and forever.

Like Moriah, Calvary displays a costly promise fulfilled—the promise that, through Abraham's seed, all the nations of the world would be blessed.

Like Sinai, Calvary inaugurates a new era of God's working in the world—no longer lived in the shadow of Mosaic law but in the brilliant wonder of amazing grace.

Like Nebo, Calvary shows that sin has consequences— but Jesus himself took those consequences on himself in our place.

Like Zion, Calvary was the place where the King of Kings was enthroned on the cross to make the ancient city of kings His own.

Like Carmel, Calvary is the place where God calls us to return to Him, forsaking our sin and accepting His loving, forgiving welcome.

Like the mount of teaching, Calvary displays the King living out the kingdom ethic of loving your enemies— even at the greatest cost imaginable.

Like the Mount of Transfiguration, Calvary shows the King in His glory—lifted up so that all people could be drawn to Him.

Calvary is not merely the continuation of the story told by these other mountains: it is the absolute culmination and fulfillment of that story as well. There on Calvary, the eternal purposes of a loving, heavenly Father were accomplished— at the greatest cost. Such love deserves the response of our whole hearts in worship and wonder, as expressed by Charles Gabriel in his classic hymn "My Savior's Love":

I stand amazed in the presence
Of Jesus the Nazarene,
And wonder how He could love me,
A sinner, condemned, unclean.

He took my sins and my sorrows,
He made them His very own;
He bore the burden to Calv'ry,
And suffered and died alone.

How marvelous! How wonderful!
And my song shall ever be:
How marvelous! How wonderful!
Is my Savior's love for me!

Calvary, where the love of God was fully and ultimately displayed, is truly the highest place.

Go, Tell It on the Mountains

Of course, the story does not end on Calvary, for there are more mountains to come, for the cross is not the final chapter in this momentous story. On the third day, from the Garden Tomb near Calvary, Jesus rose from the grave in the divine exclamation that death had lost the battle. The eyewitnesses of the risen Christ—and the startling transformation the resurrection made upon them—became a force that, eventually, was accused of turning the world upside down (Acts 17:6 NKJV). And, in that transformation, more mountains played a part.

The Mount of Olives, where earlier Jesus made His triumphal entry into Jerusalem (Matthew 21:1), was also the place where our Lord gave His final of five discourses recorded in Matthew (chapters 23–25). That same Mount of Olives was the site where, forty days after His resurrection, Jesus ascended back to the presence of His Father (Acts 1:9–10).

There is also Mars Hill, the ancient Athenian "think tank" where Paul, in a brilliant contextualization of the message of Jesus into Grecian culture, presented the story of that very same resurrection to the scholars and intellectuals of the Greek capital (Acts 17). To ancient Greeks who largely saw the physical body as evil and irredeemable, the thought of a physical resurrection would have sent shock waves through some of the most brilliant minds of their generation.

> The same Jesus who ascended from the Mount of Olives will one day return.

And, yes, there were the seven hills of Rome—the political and military center of the ancient Mediterranean world—where the followers of Jesus lived out their faith in, arguably, the most hostile environment the church has ever faced. Where tradition says that Simon Peter eventually kept his promise to die for Jesus (Luke 22:33). Where Paul likewise died for the gospel.

Mountains continued to play their part in the biblical story of God's costly rescue of His broken creation. And there is the reminder that the same Jesus who ascended from the Mount of Olives will one day return. This return was promised by two angelic beings who joined the dumbstruck disciples who saw Jesus depart from the mount:

> They said, "Men of Galilee, why do you stand looking into the sky? This Jesus, who has been taken up from you into heaven, will come in the same way as you have watched Him go into heaven." (Acts 1:11)

Yet that promised return wasn't exactly new news. Centuries earlier, the prophet Zechariah promised that Israel's Messiah would come to that very place—the Mount of Olives:

> And his feet shall stand in that day upon the mount of Olives, which is before Jerusalem on the east, and the mount of Olives shall cleave in the midst thereof toward the east and toward the west, and there shall be a very great valley; and half of the mountain shall remove toward the north, and half of it toward the south. (Zechariah 14:4 KJV)

Mountains help to tell the Bible story from beginning to end. But what about the end? Perhaps one final Old Testament prophecy remains for us to consider, for it speaks powerfully of what will happen when the one true King *does* return to rule and to reign:

> Let every valley be lifted up,
> And every mountain and hill be made low;
> And let the uneven ground become a plain,
> And the rugged terrain a broad valley. (Isaiah 40:4)

Why is that important? *The Bible Knowledge Commentary* explains:

> Raising the valleys and lowering the mountains refer in hyperbole to workmen leveling or smoothing out the roads on which a dignitary would travel when he came to visit an area. Today an equivalent is, "roll out the red carpet." In Isaiah's day he was calling Israel to be "smoothed out" so that the Lord could come to

the nation and rule. This was emphasized by all the prophets—ethically the nation must be righteous. Eventually the nation will be "smoothed out" spiritually when the glory of the LORD is revealed (Isa. 40:5).

Every mountain will be made low. Why?

I would argue that the mountains which played such a major role in telling the story of the King will no longer be needed.

The King will be here at last.

As Isaac Watts wrote:

Joy to the world! the Lord is come;
Let earth receive her King;
Let every heart prepare him room,
And heaven and nature sing,
And heaven and nature sing,
And heaven, and heaven, and nature sing.

Help us get the word out!

Our Daily Bread Publishing exists to feed the soul with the Word of God.

If you appreciated this book, please let others know.

- Pick up another copy to give as a gift.
- Share a link to the book or mention it on social media.
- Write a review on your blog, on a book-seller's website, or at our own site (odb.org/store).
- Recommend this book for your church, book club, or small group.

Connect with us:

[f] @ourdailybread

[IG] @ourdailybread

[t] @ourdailybread

Our Daily Bread Publishing
PO Box 3566
Grand Rapids, Michigan 49501 USA

[✉] books@odb.org